Modest
MUSSORGSKY

NIGHT ON BALD MOUNTAIN
FANTASY FOR ORCHESTRA

Arranged by

Nikolay Rimsky-Korsakov

Edited by

Clinton F. Nieweg

Full Score
Partitur

PETRUCCI LIBRARY PRESS

During the season of 1882-3 I continued working on *Khovanshchina* and other compositions of Moussorgsky's. *A Night on Bald Mountain* was the only thing I could not find my way with. Originally composed in the sixties—under the influence of Liszt's *Todtentanz*—for the piano with accompaniment of orchestra, this piece (then called *St. John's Eve* and both severely and justly criticized by Balakirev) had long been utterly neglected by its author, gathering dust among his unfinished works. When composing Gedeonov's *Mlada*, Moussorgsky had made use of the material to be found in *A Night on Bald Mountain* and, introducing singing into it, had written the scene of Chernobog on Mount Triglav (Three Peaks). That was the second form of the same piece in substance. Its third form had developed in his composing of *The Fair at Sorochintsy*, when Moussorgsky conceived the queer and incoherent idea of making the peasant lad, without rhyme or reason, see the Witches' Sabbath in a dream; this was to form a sort of stage intermezzo that did not chime at all with the rest of the scenario of *Sorochinskaya Yarmarka*. This time the piece ended with the ringing of the village church bell, at the sounds of which the frightened evil spirits vanished. Tranquillity and dawn were built on the theme of the peasant lad himself, who had seen the fantastic dream. In working on Moussorgsky's piece I made use of its last version for the purpose of closing the composition. Now then, the first form of the piece was for piano solo with orchestra; the second form and the third, vocal compositions and for the stage, into the bargain (unorchestrated)! None of these forms was fit to be published and performed. With Moussorgsky's material as a basis I decided to create an instrumental piece, by retaining all of the author's best and coherent material, adding the fewest possible interpolations of my own. It was necessary to create a form in which Moussorgsky's ideas would mould in the best fashion. It was a difficult task, of which the satisfactory solution baffled me for two years, though in the other works of Moussorgsky I had got on with comparative ease. I had been uable to get at either form, modulation, or orchestration; and the piece lay inert until the following year.

. . . The orchestration of *A Night on Bald Mountain*, which had baffled me so long was finished for the concerts of [the 1886-7] season, and the piece, [conducted] by me at the first concert in a manner that could not be improved upon, was demanded again and again with unanimity.

Nikolai Rimsky-Korsakov, *My musical life*

"Subterranean sounds from supernatural voices.—Appearance of
the spirits of the dark and, after them, of Chernobog (the black
god).—Glorification of Chernobog and Black Mass.—Sabbath.—At
the height of the sabbath, distant echo of the bell of a small village
church; this disperses the spirits of the dark.—The break of day".

From Mussorgsky's autograph manuscript

ORCHESTRA

Piccolo

2 Flutes

2 Oboes

2 Clarinets (B-flat and A)

2 Bassoons

4 Horns (F)

2 Trumpets (B-flat)

3 Trombones

Tuba

Timpani

Percussion

Cymbals, Bass Drum, Tam-Tam

Low Bell (D)

Harp

Violins I

Violins II

Violas

Cellos

Double Basses

Duration: ca.10 minutes

First performance: October 15, 1886
St. Petersburg, Kononov Hall
RSC Orchestra, Nikolay Rimsky-Korsakov (conductor)

ISMN: 979-0-58021-251-1

NIGHT ON BALD MOUNTAIN

Completed and orchestrated by
Nikolay Rimsky Korsakov

Modest Mussorgsky
Edited by Clinton F. Nieweg

*) Ноэте: Арпа и Campana in D. © 1992 Clinton F. Nieweg

4

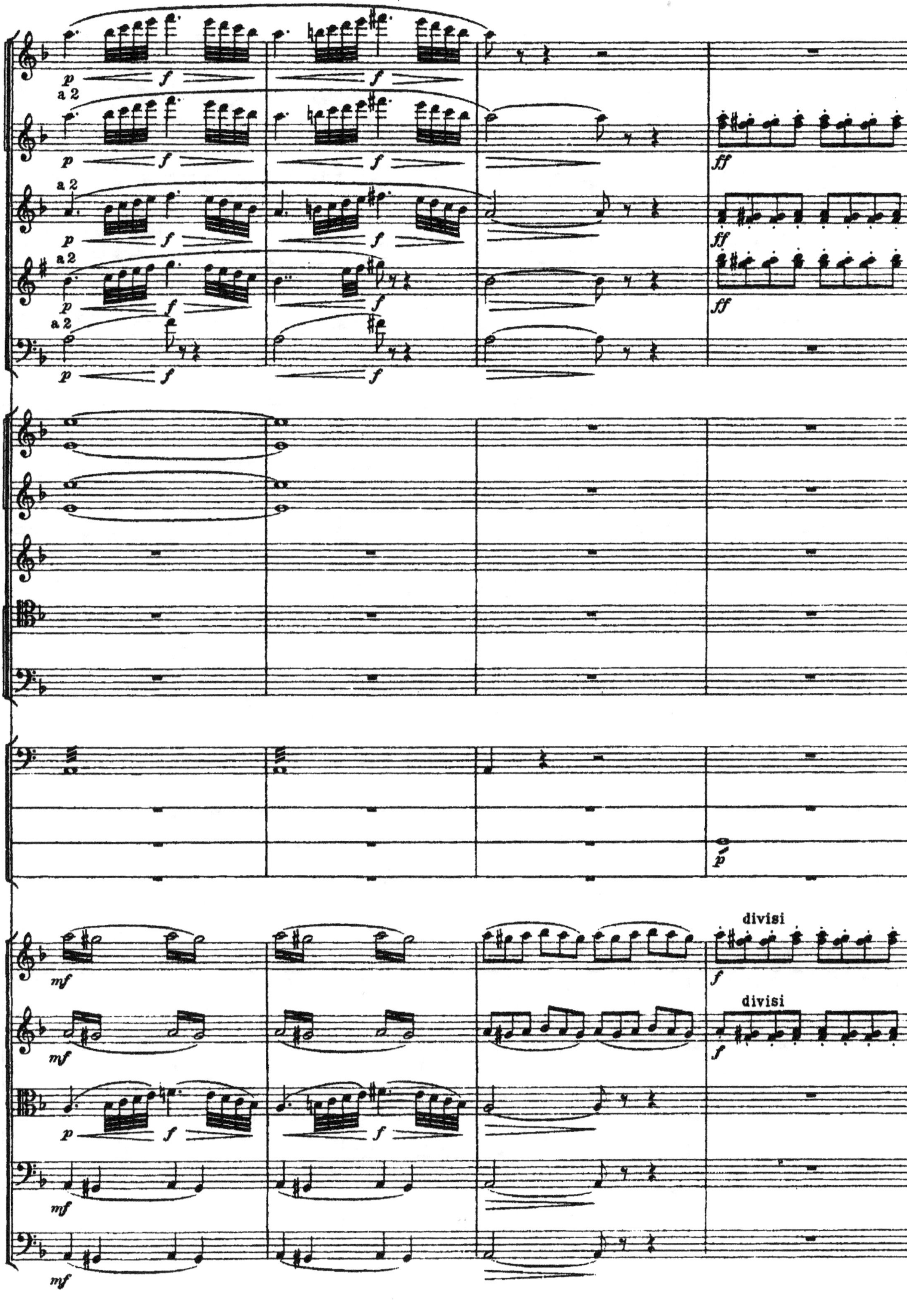
a 2
a 2
a 2
a 2
divisi
divisi

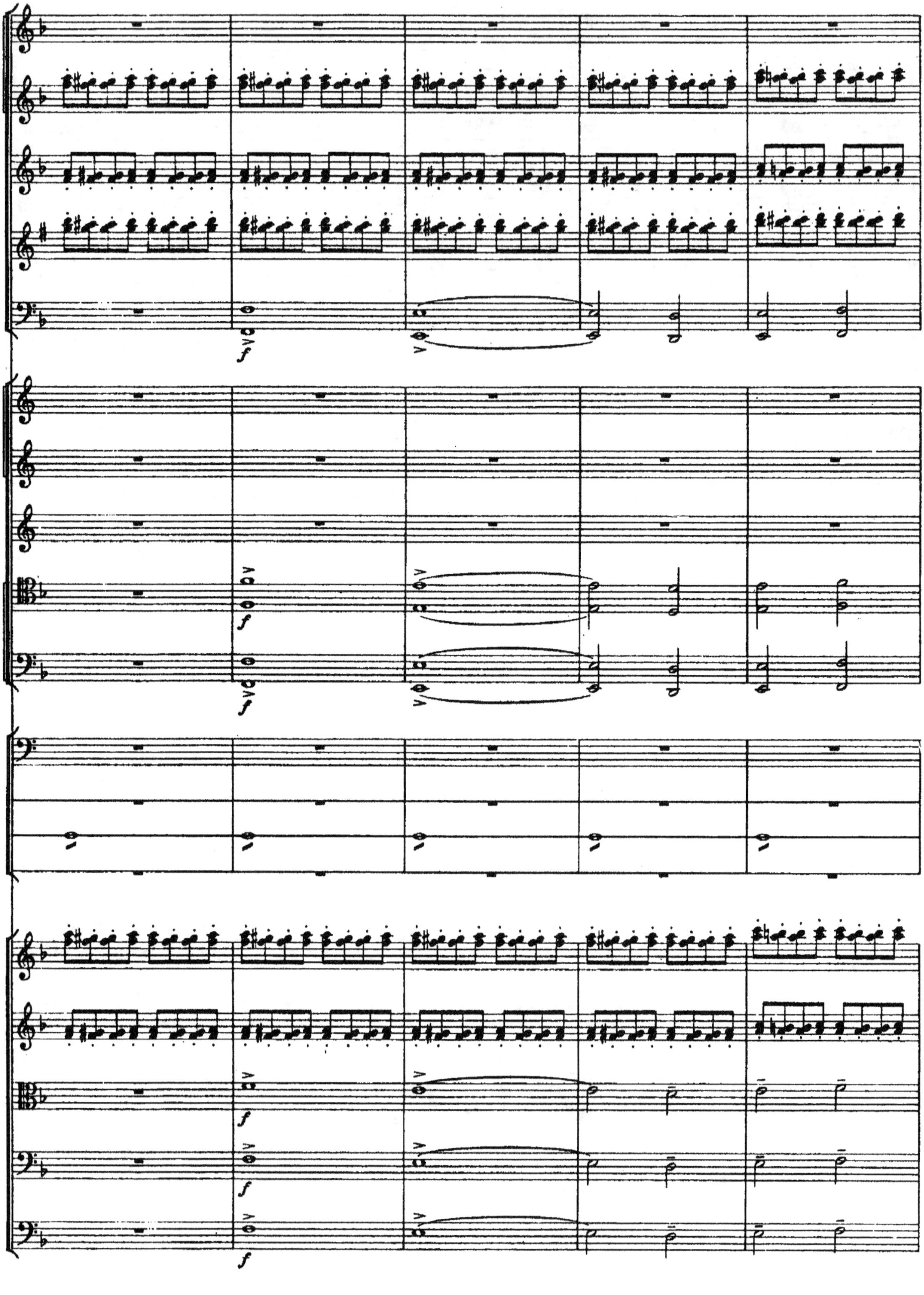

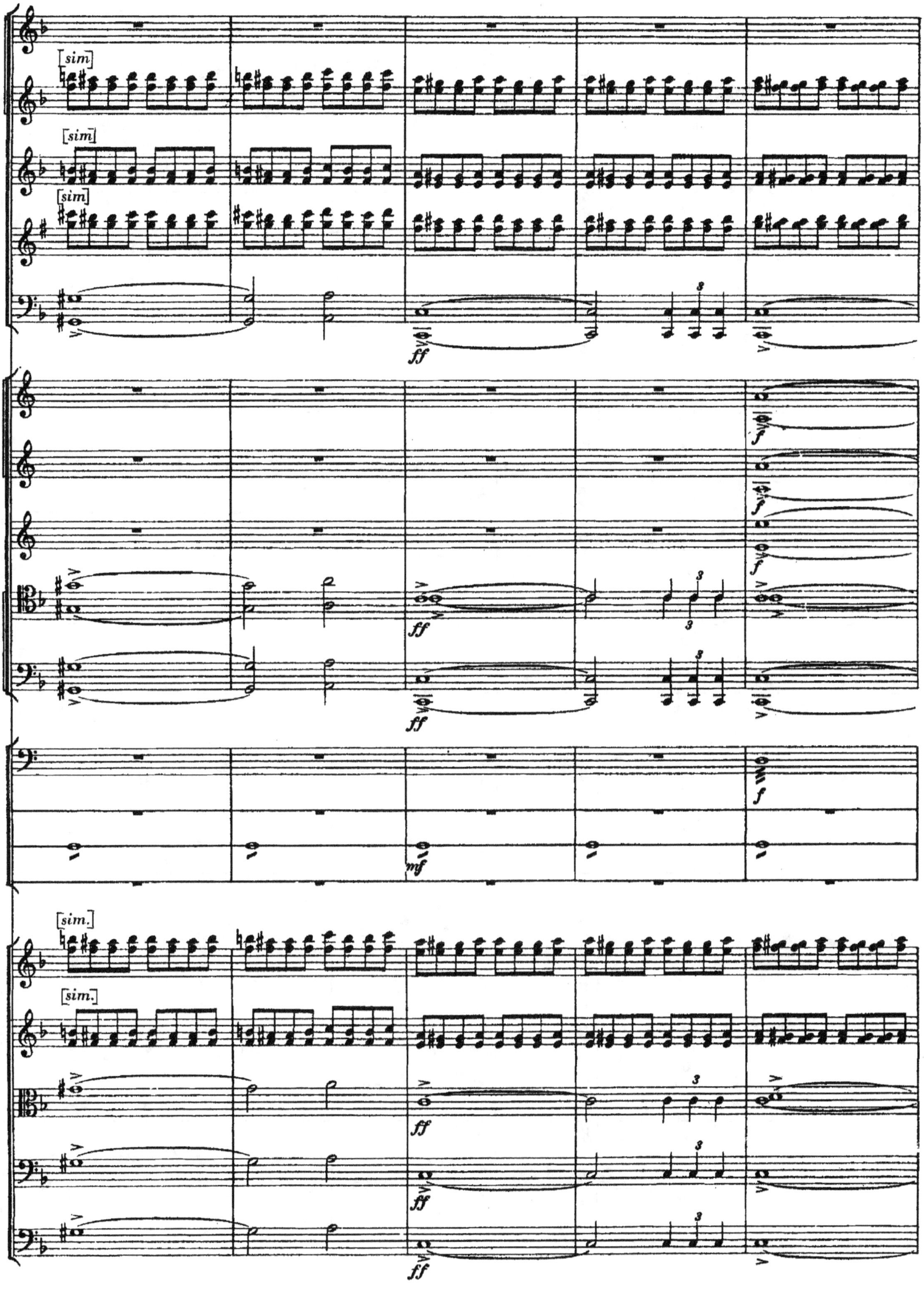
[sim]
[sim]
[sim]
ff
f
mf
[sim.]
[sim.]
3

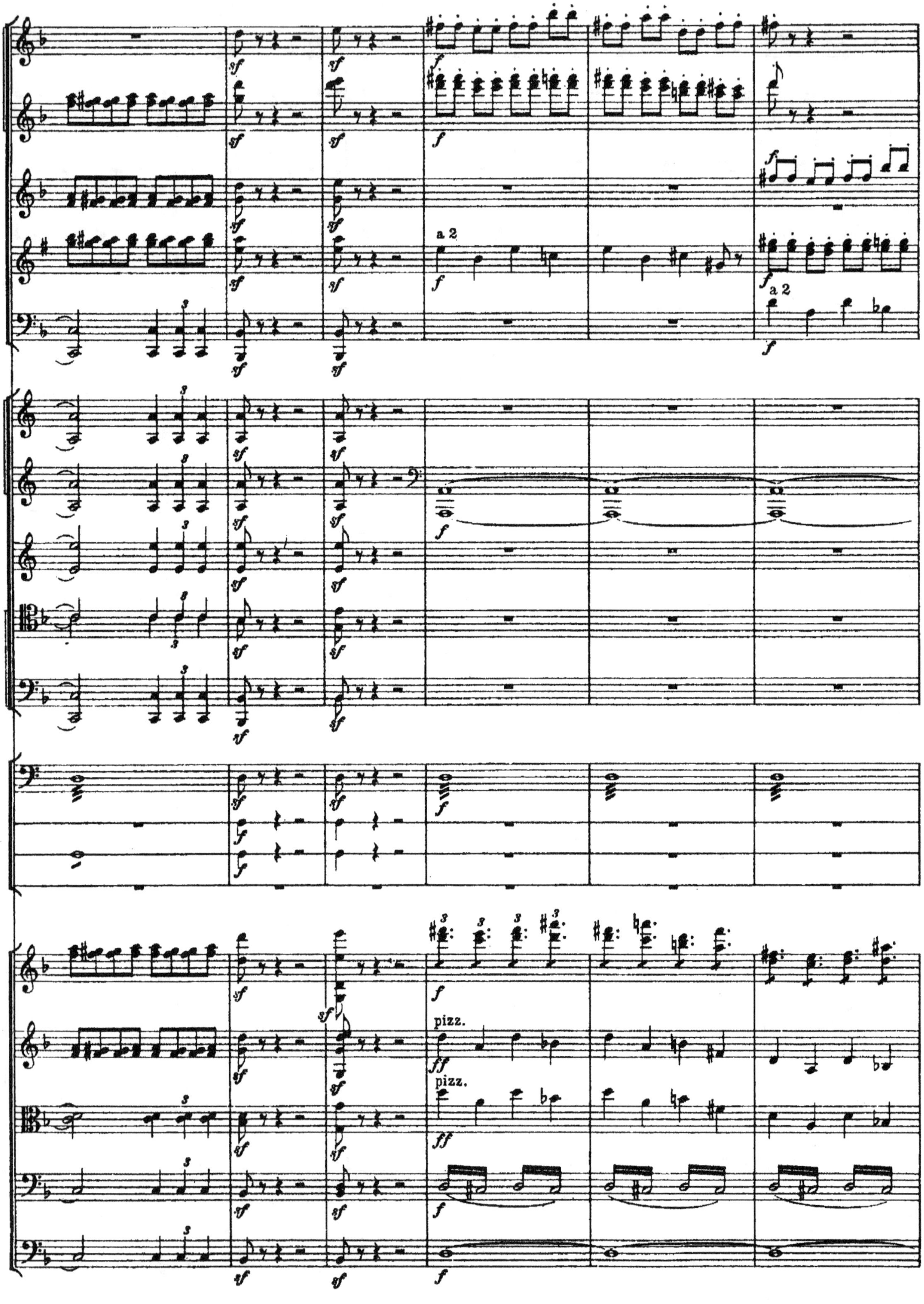
a 2
a 2
pizz.
pizz.

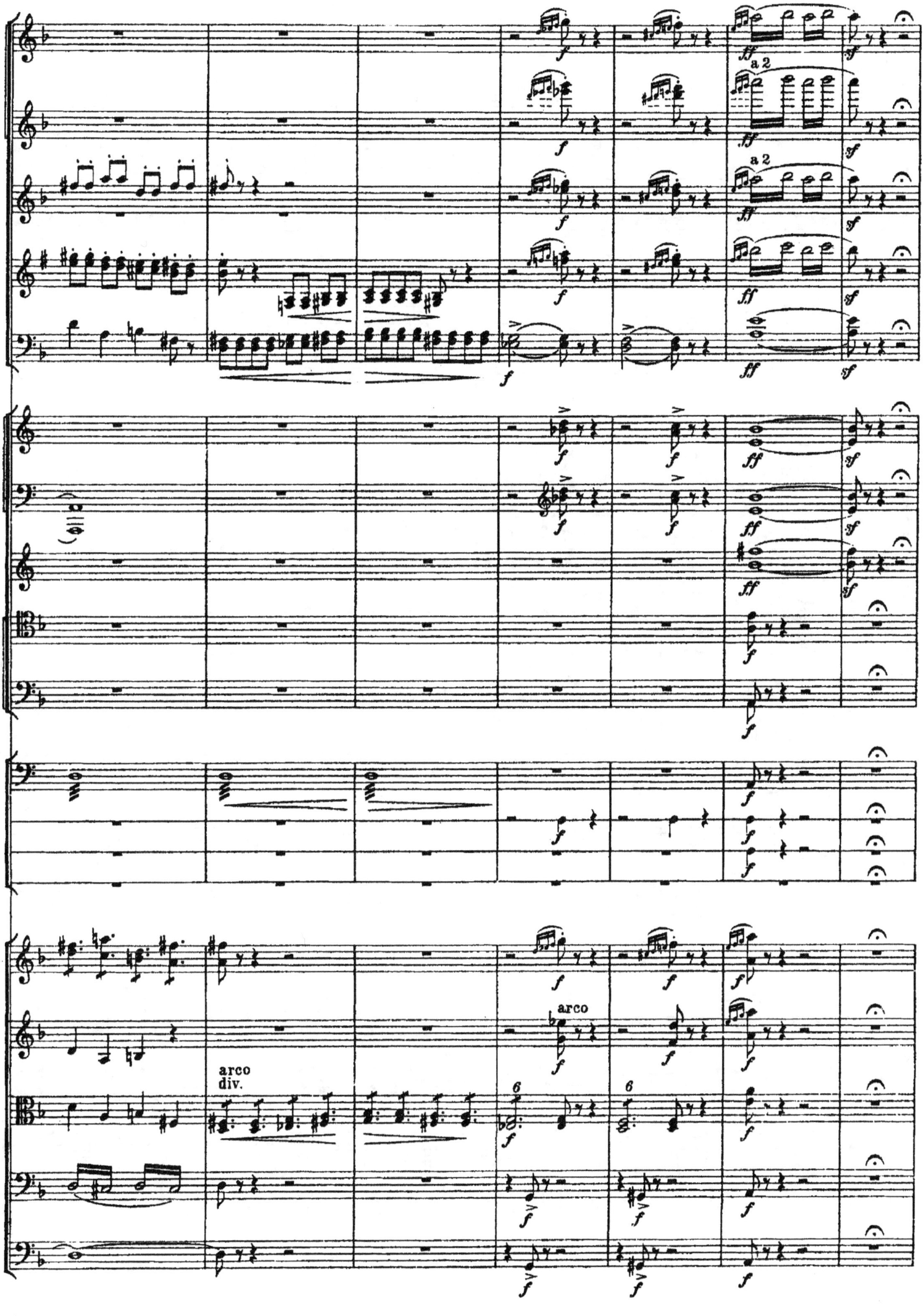
a 2
a 2
arco
div.
arco

A
Fl.
Ob.
pp cresc.
pp cresc.
pp
pp
cresc.
cresc.
pp cresc.
pp cresc.
pp cresc.
A
Fl.picc.
a 2
a 2
Clar. a 2
Fag. a 2
p
f
pp
cresc.
pp
pp cresc.
[pp]
Cor. I. II
Cor. III. IV
Timp.
p
mf
pp cresc.
pp cresc.
pp cresc.
pp cresc.
pp cresc.

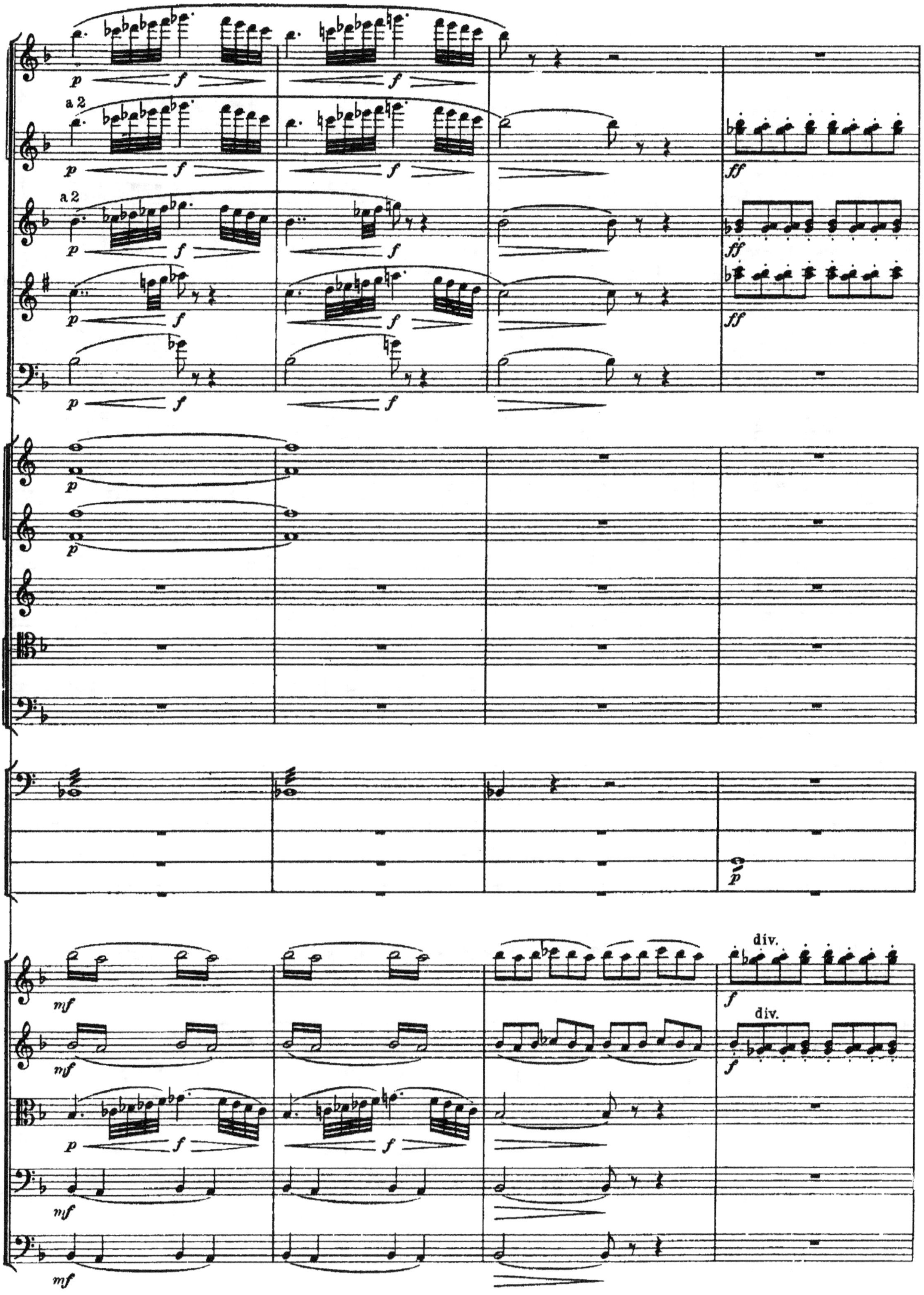
a 2
a 2
div.
div.
p
f
ff
mf

12

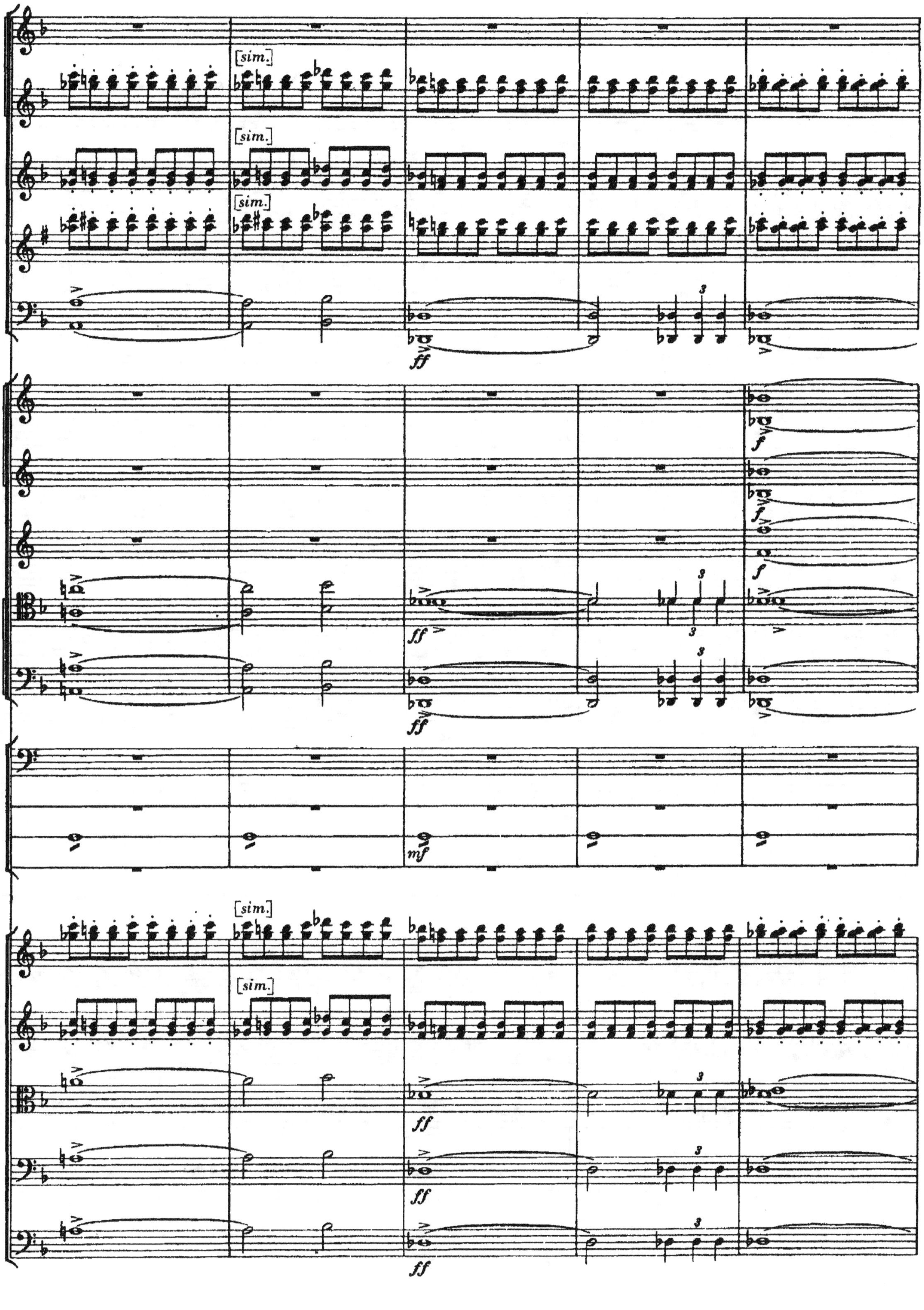
[sim.]
[sim.]
[sim.]
ff
3
f
f
f
mf
[sim.]
[sim.]
ff
ff
ff

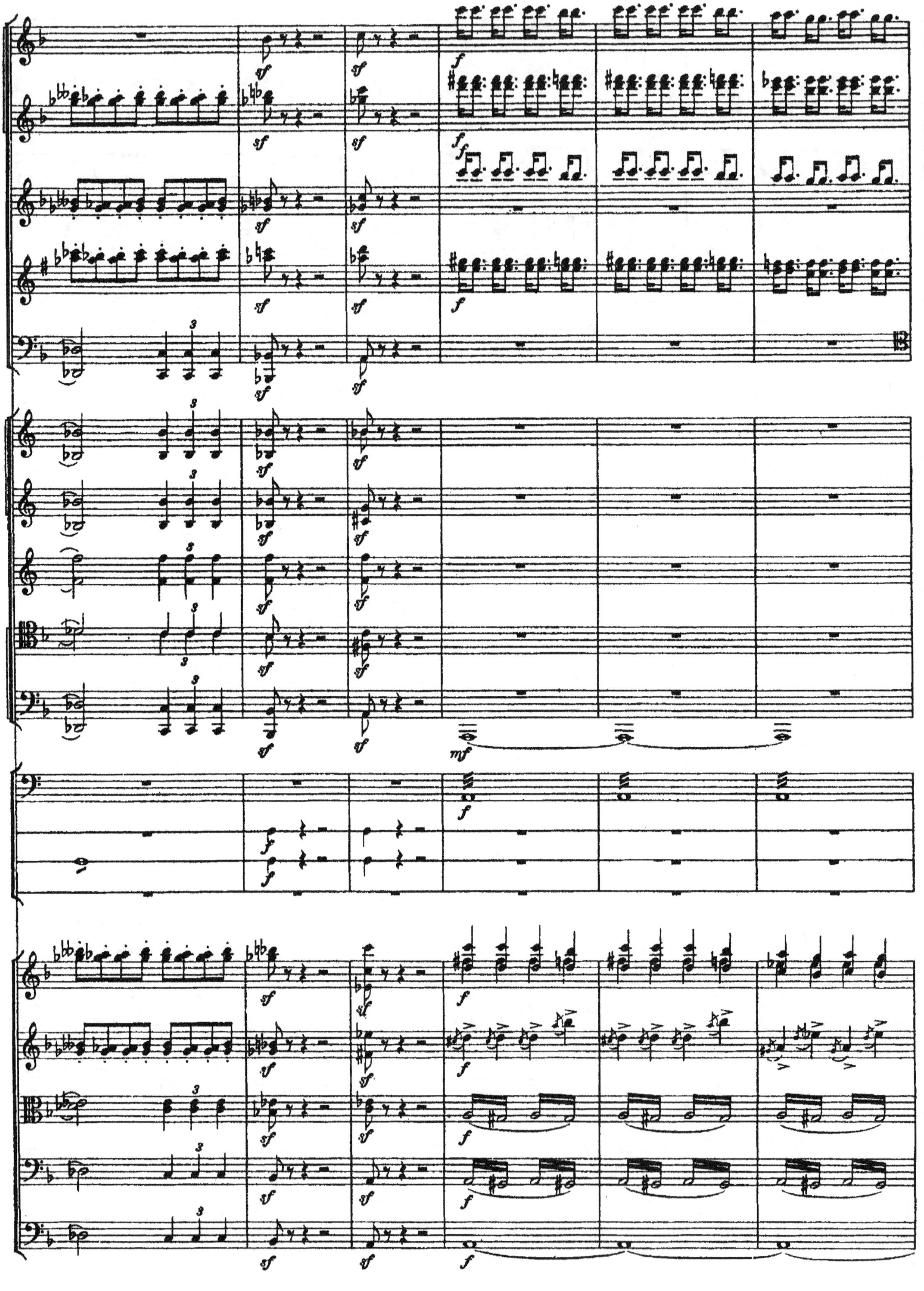

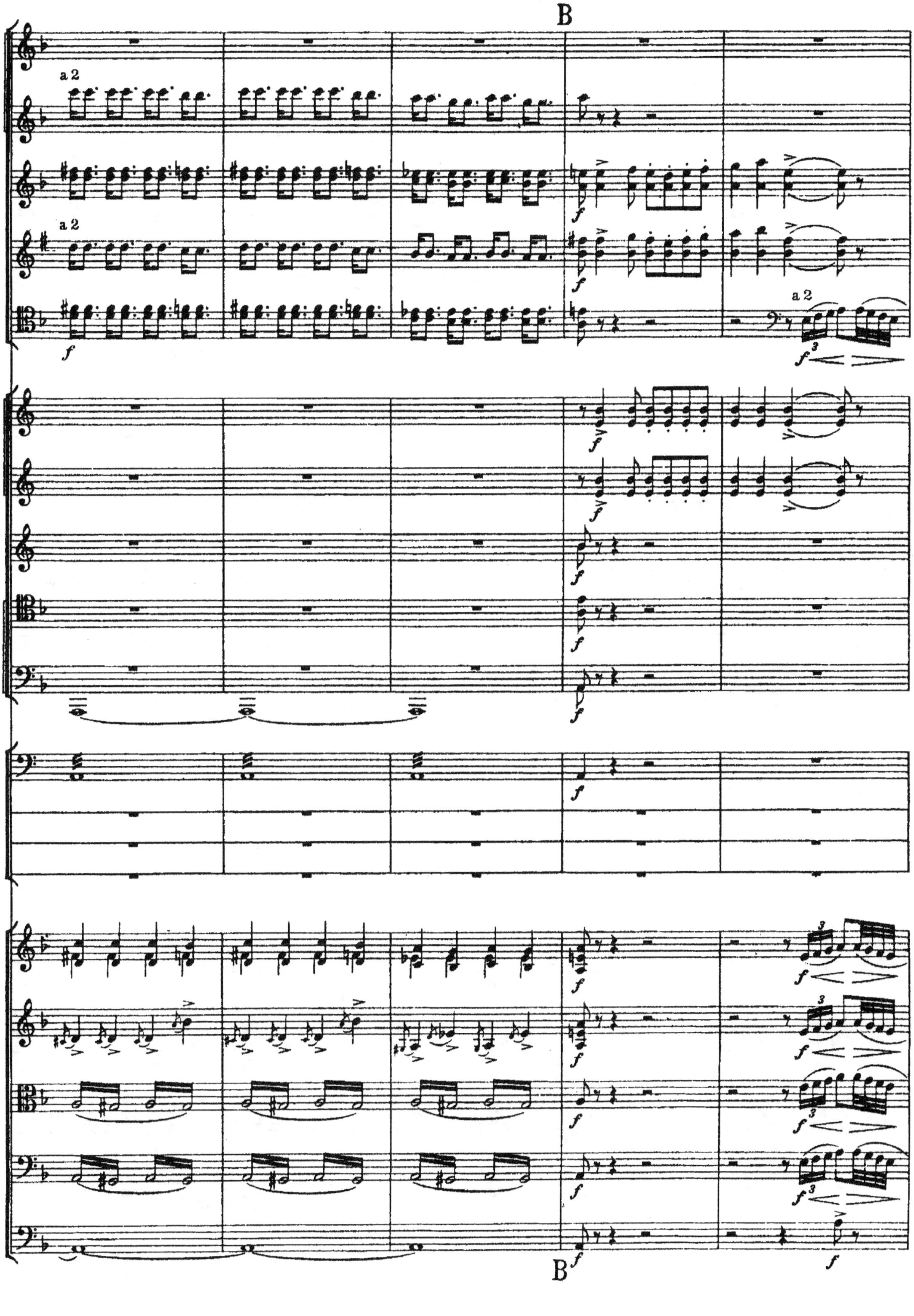
B
a 2
a 2
a 2
B

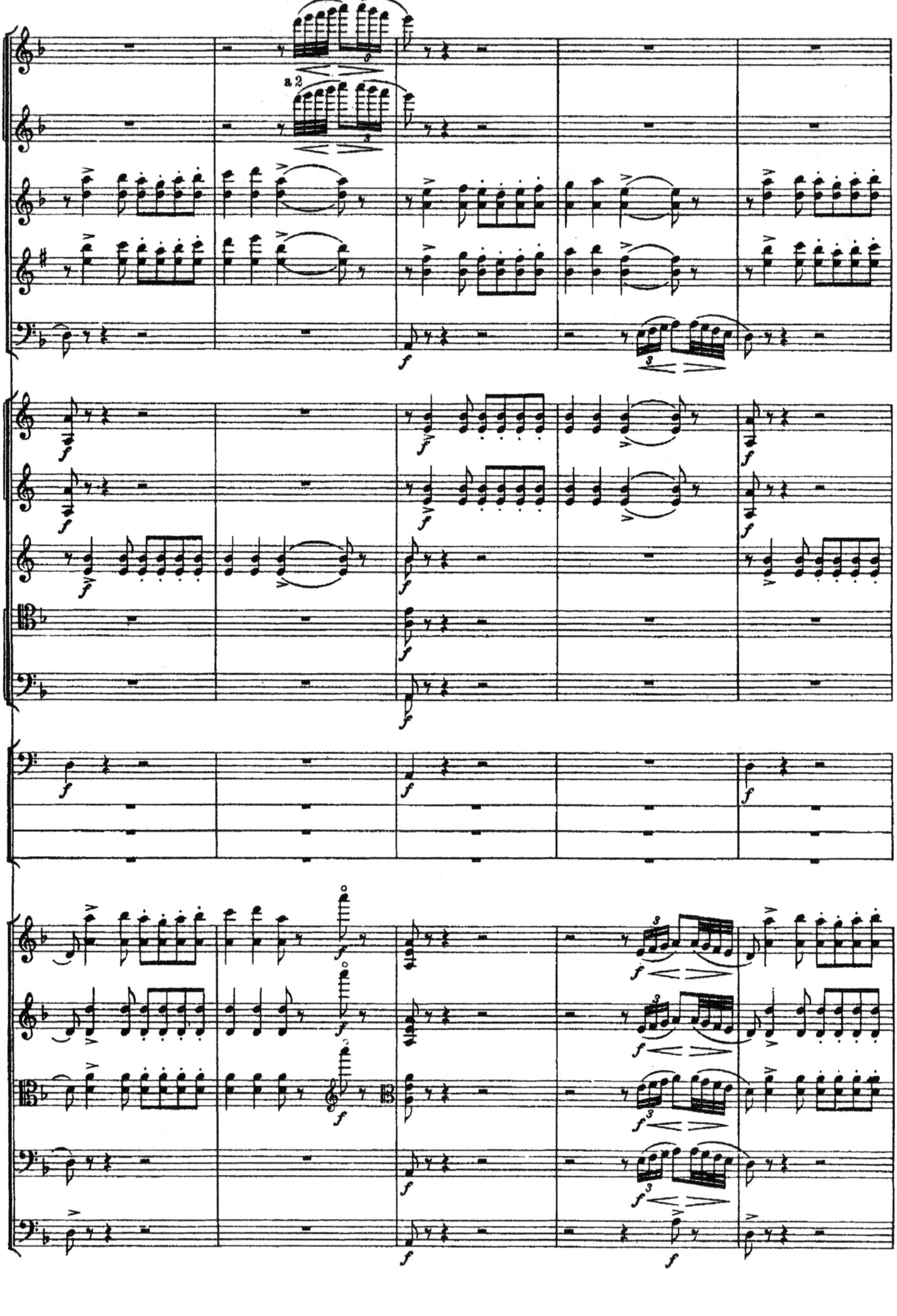
a 2

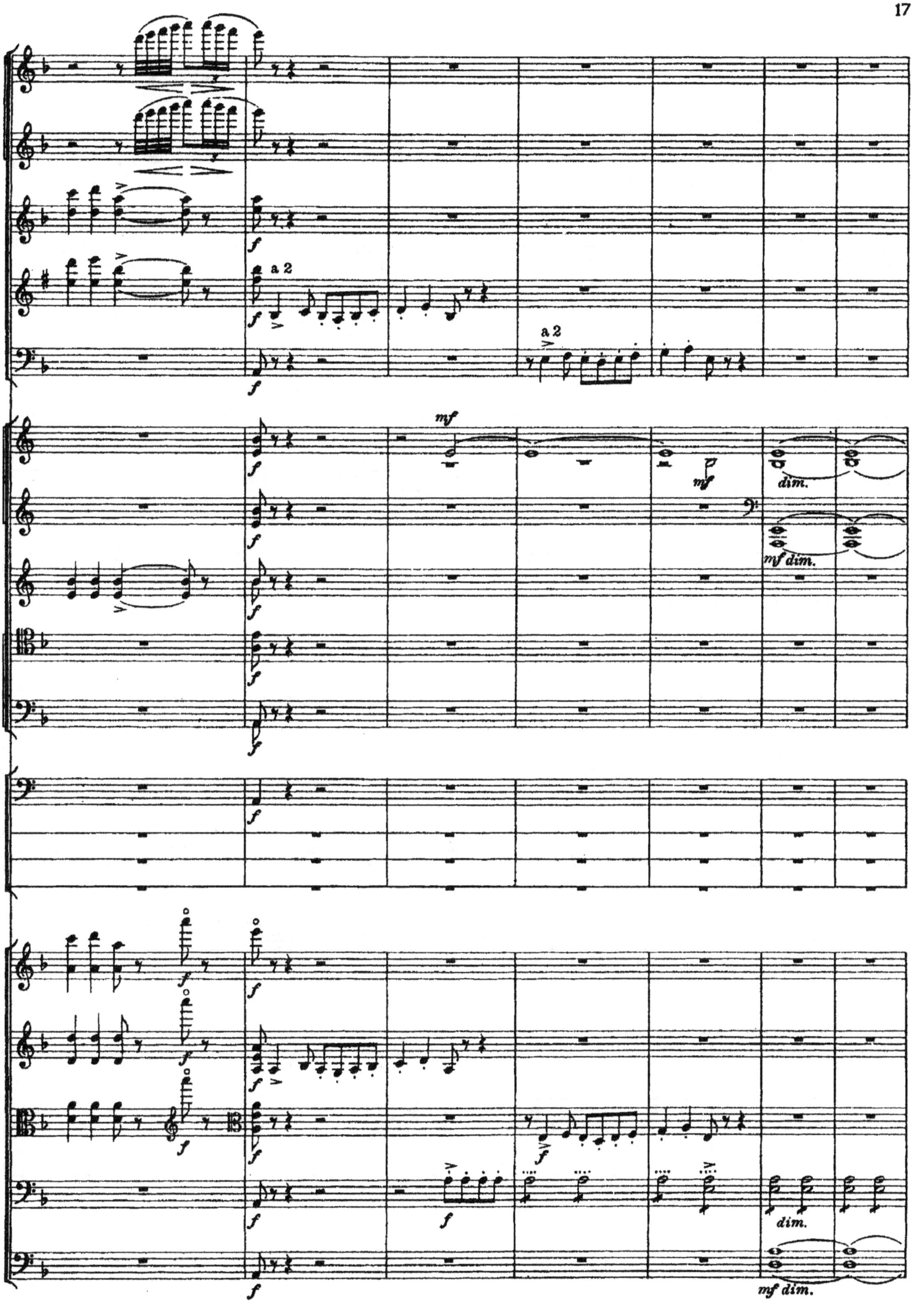
f
a 2
f
a 2
mf
mf
dim.
mf dim.
f
f
dim.
mf dim.

C

Poco più sostenuto

Poco più sostenuto

C

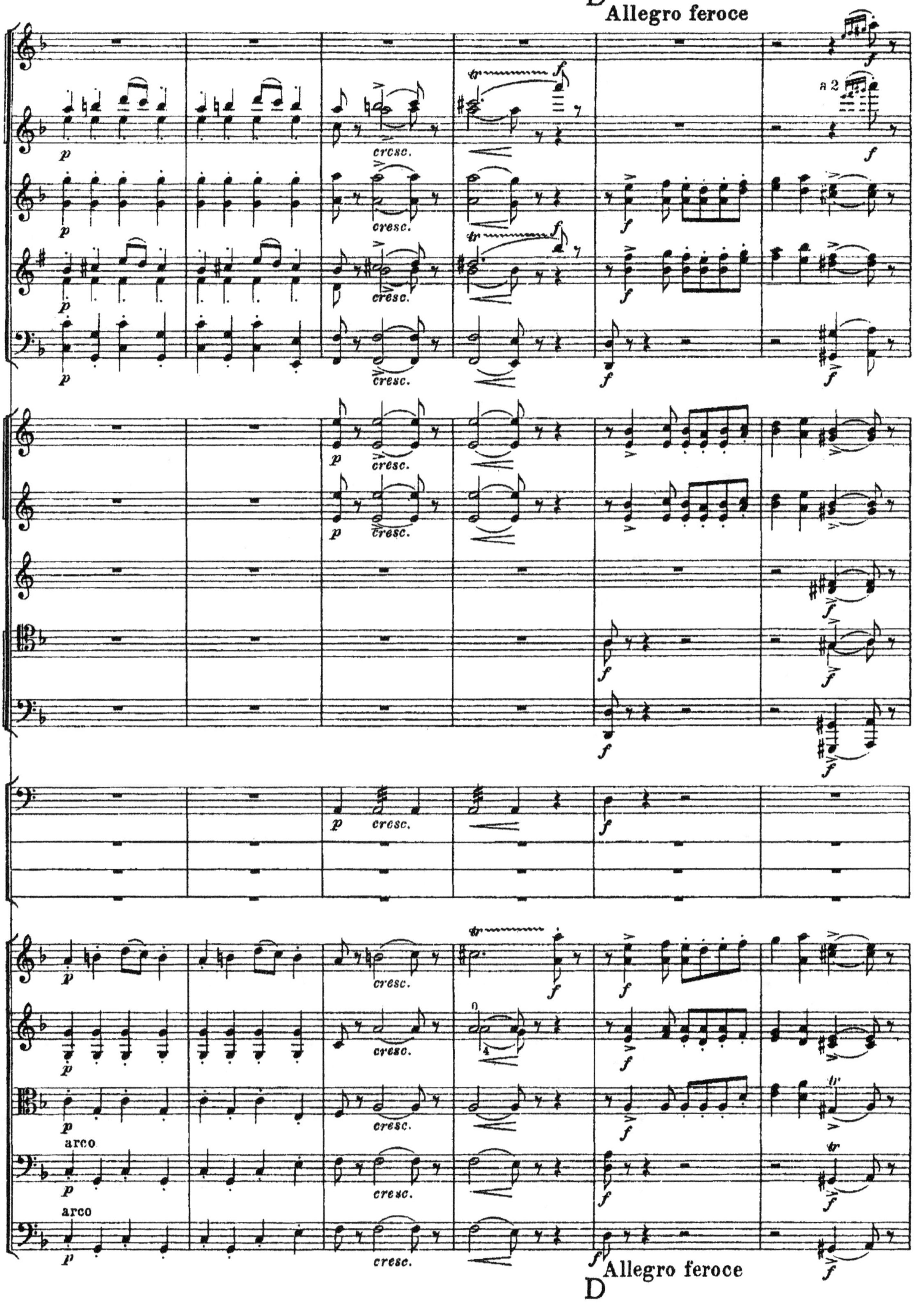
D
Allegro feroce
a 2
p
cresc.
tr
f
arco
Allegro feroce
D

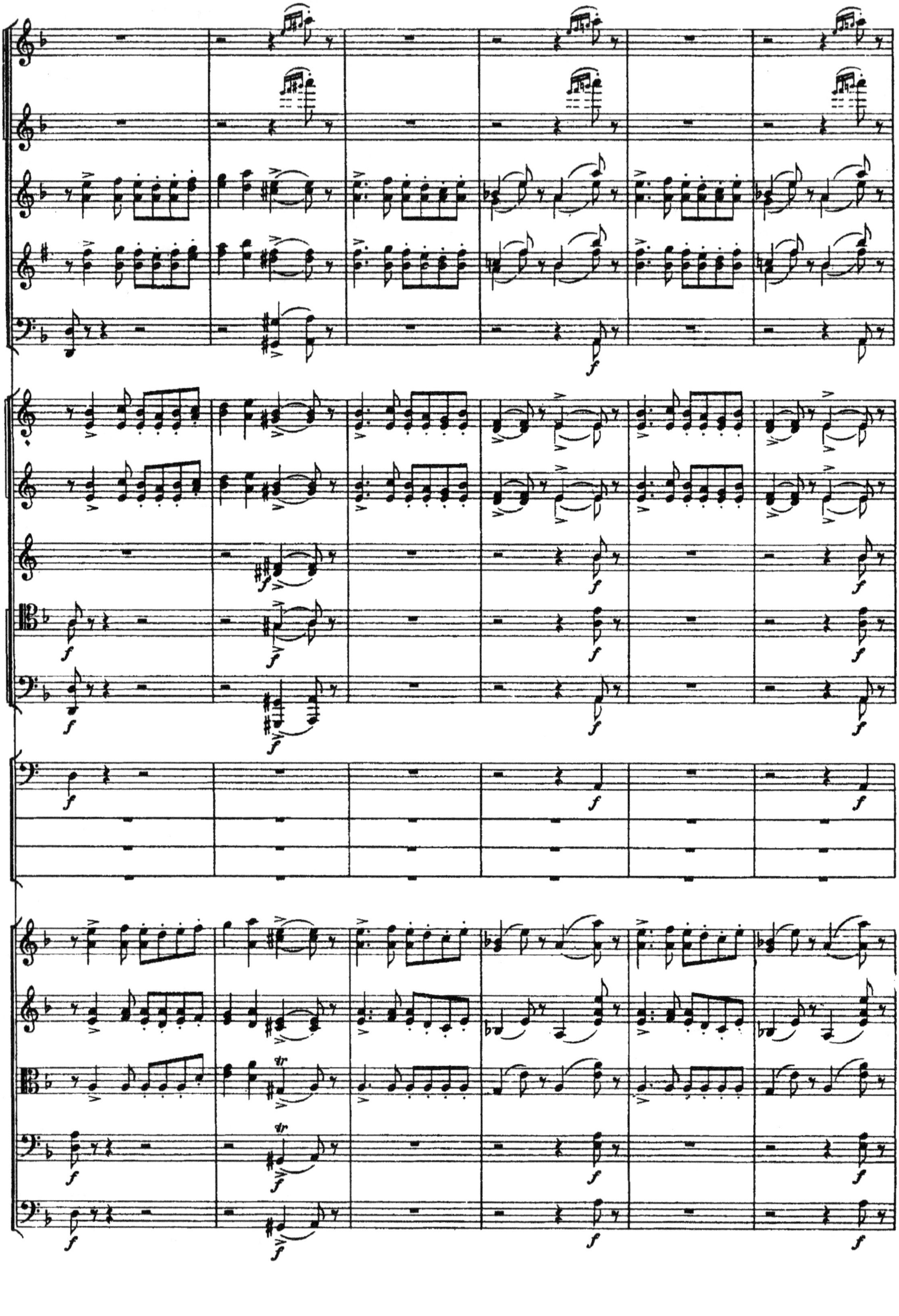

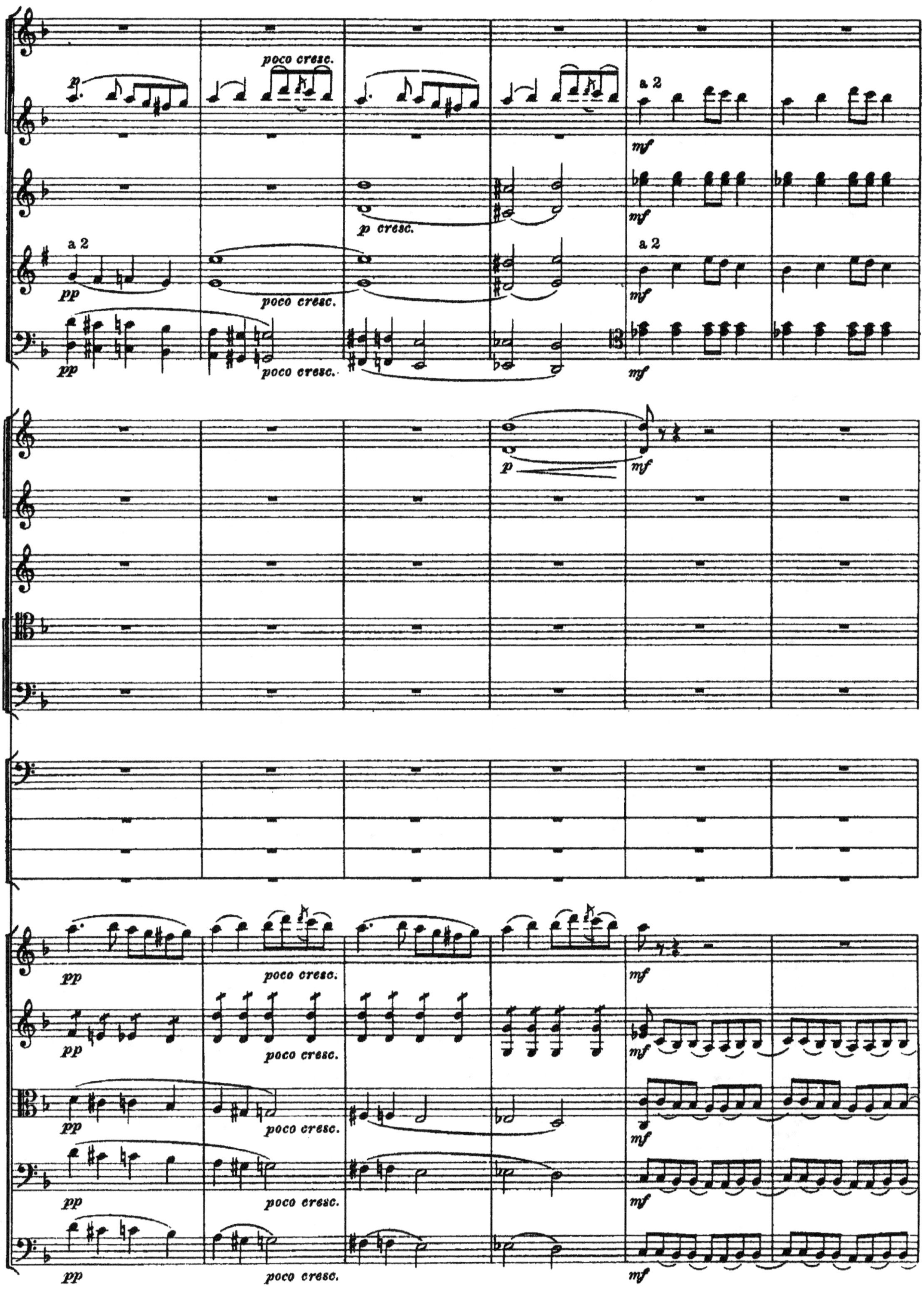
poco cresc.
a 2
p cresc.
pp
mf
p

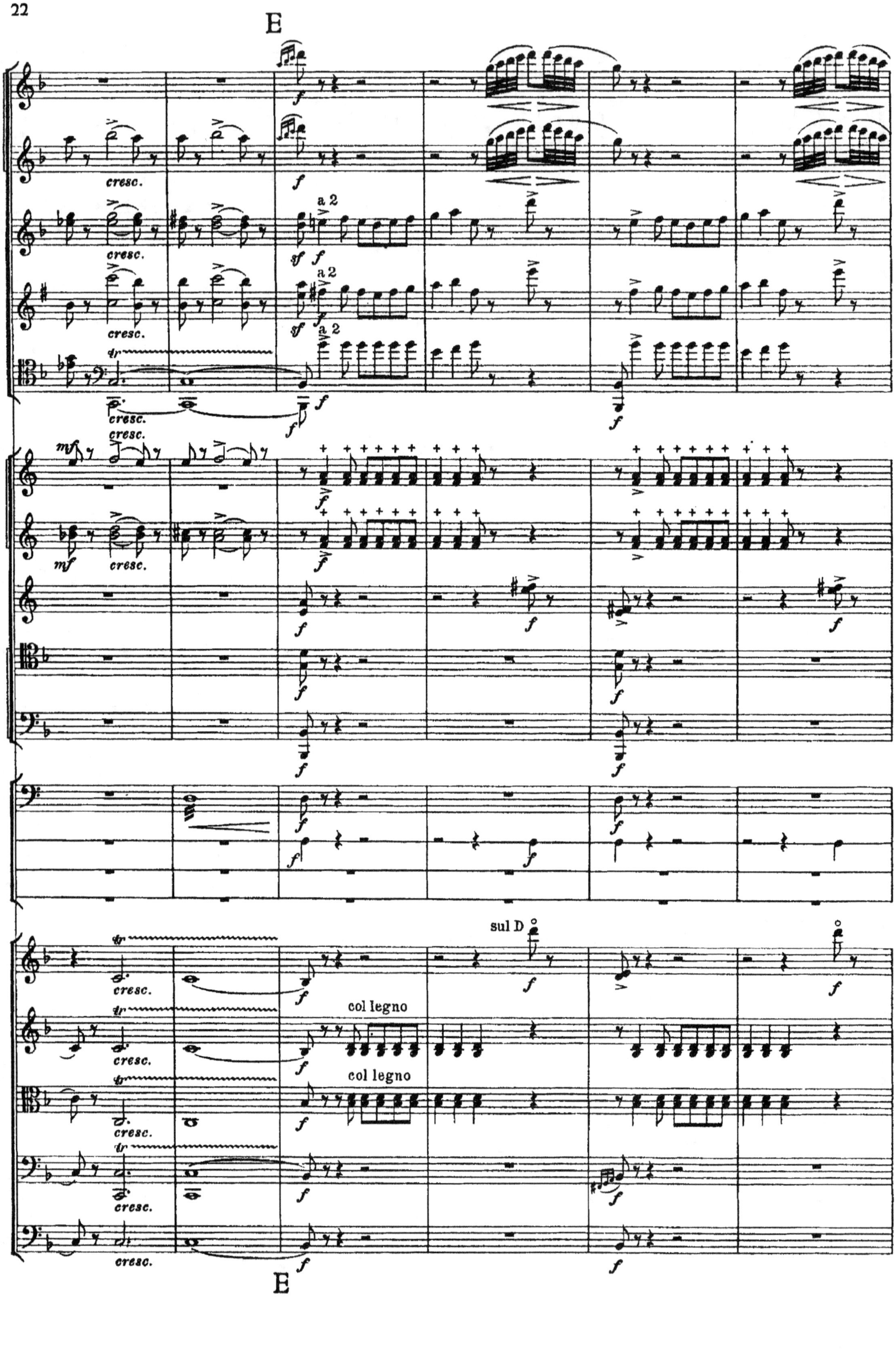
E
cresc.
a 2
tr
mf
sf
f
sul D
col legno
col legno
E

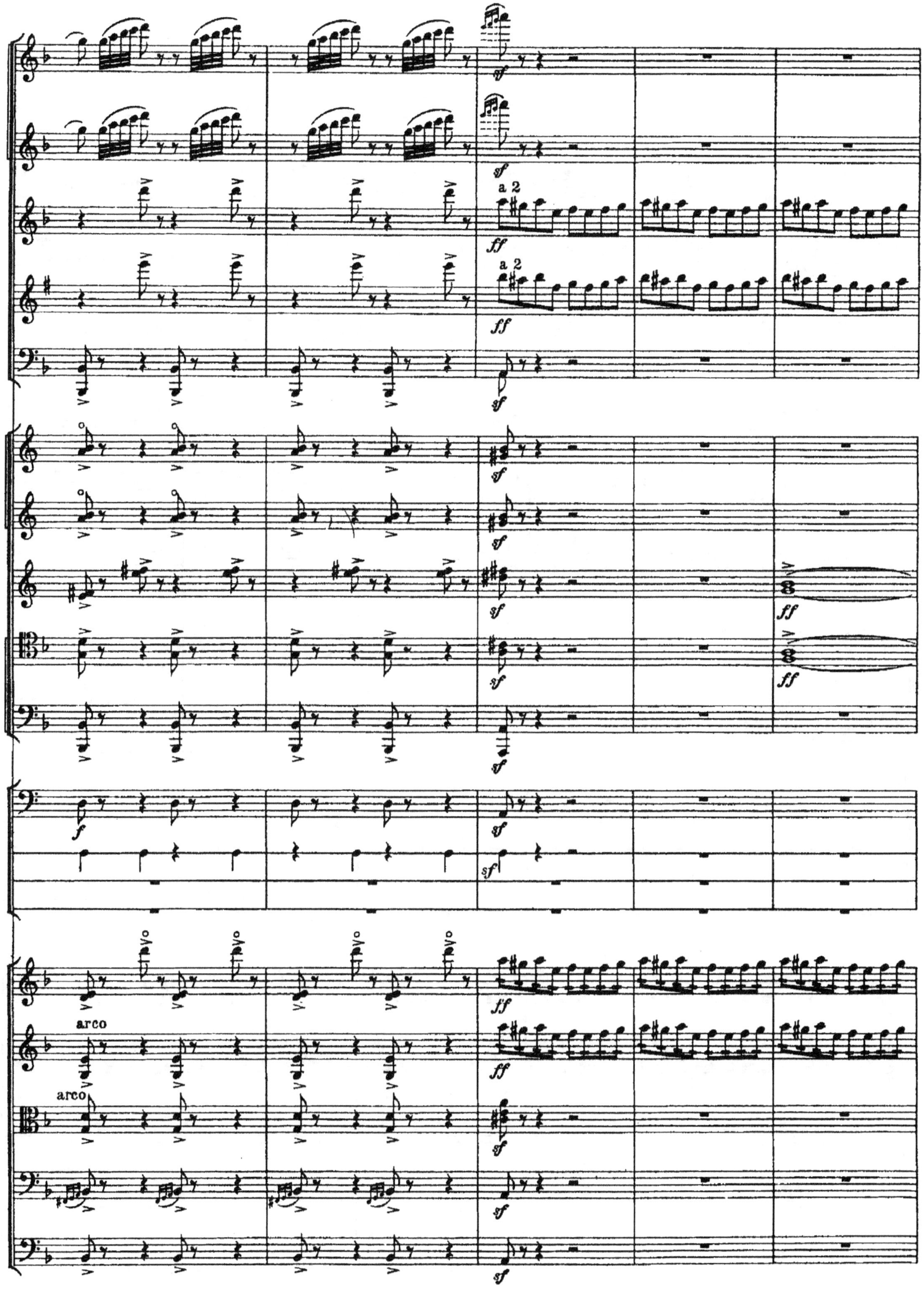
sf
a 2
ff
arco

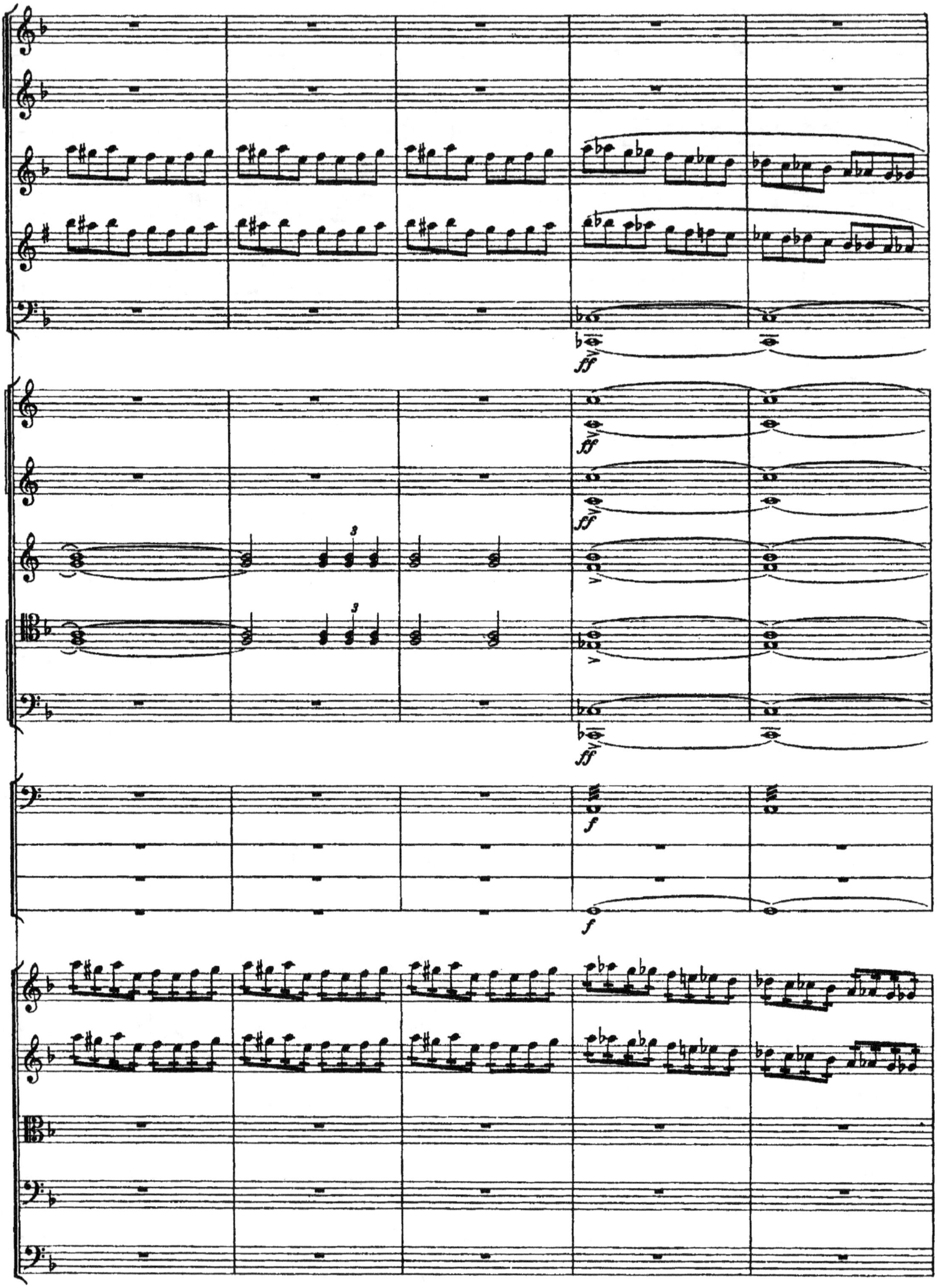
ff
ff
ff
ff
f
f

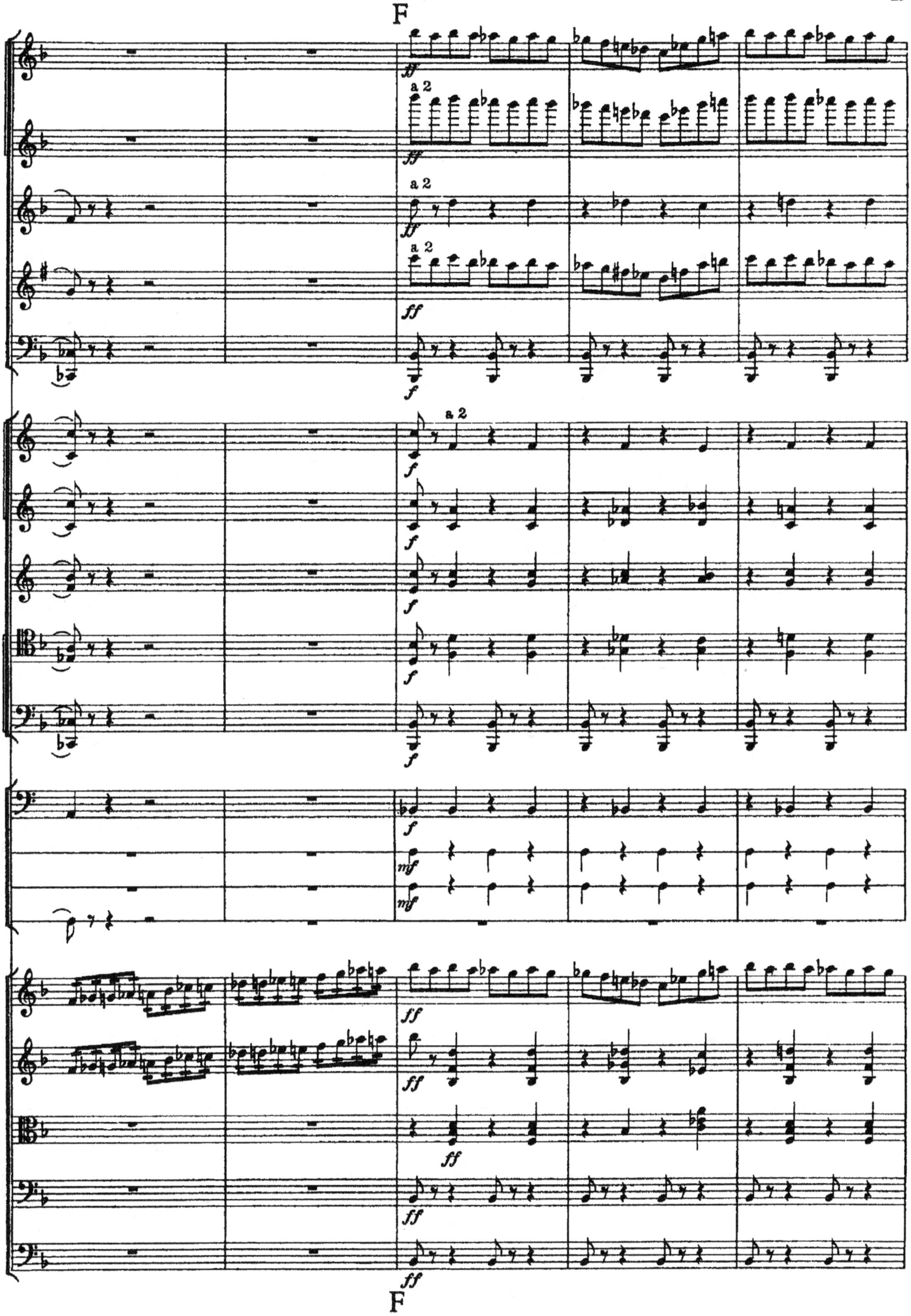
F
a 2
ff
f
mf
F

Poco più sostenuto

poco a poco più animato

poco a poco più animato

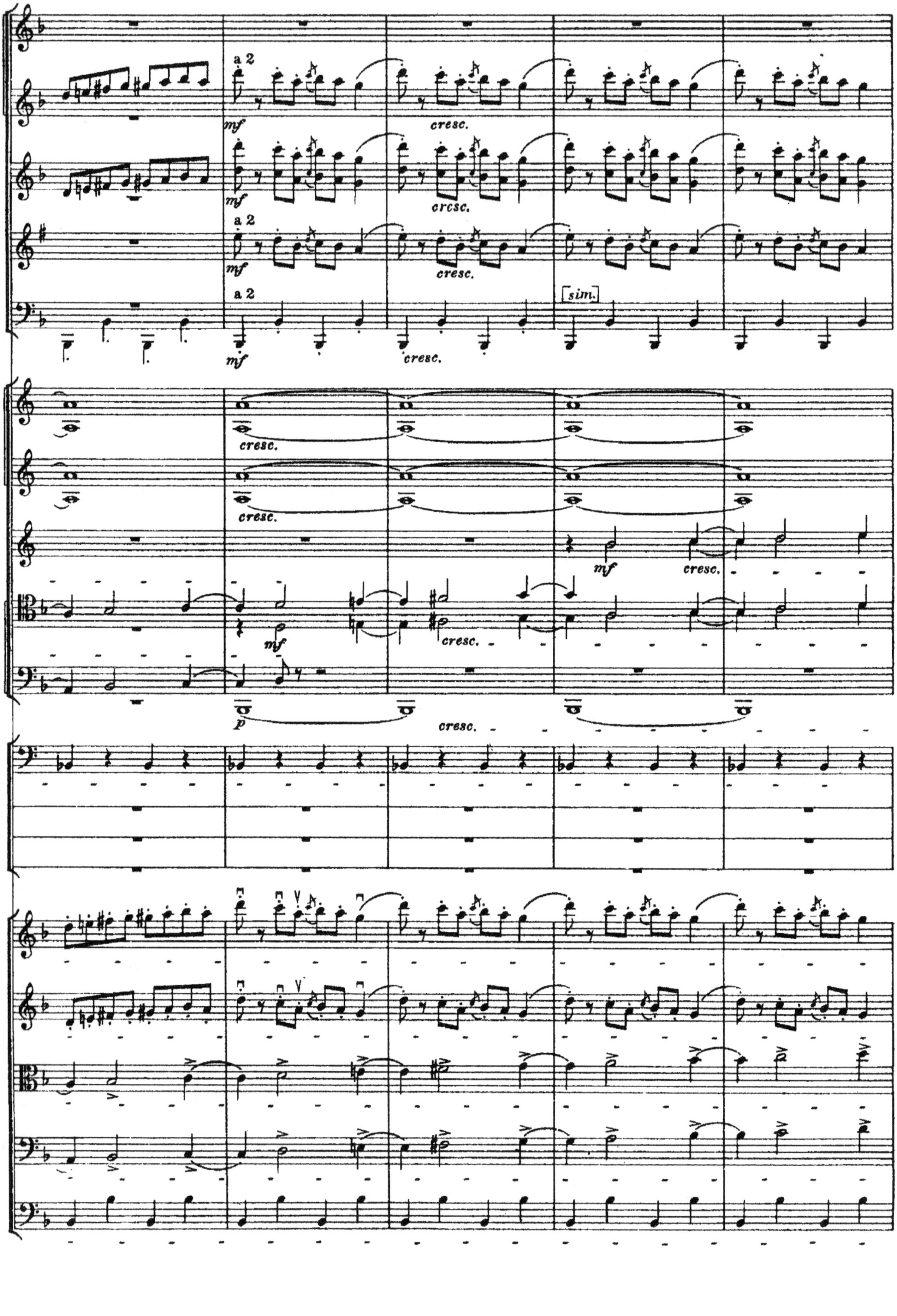
a 2
mf
cresc.
a 2
a 2
sim.
p

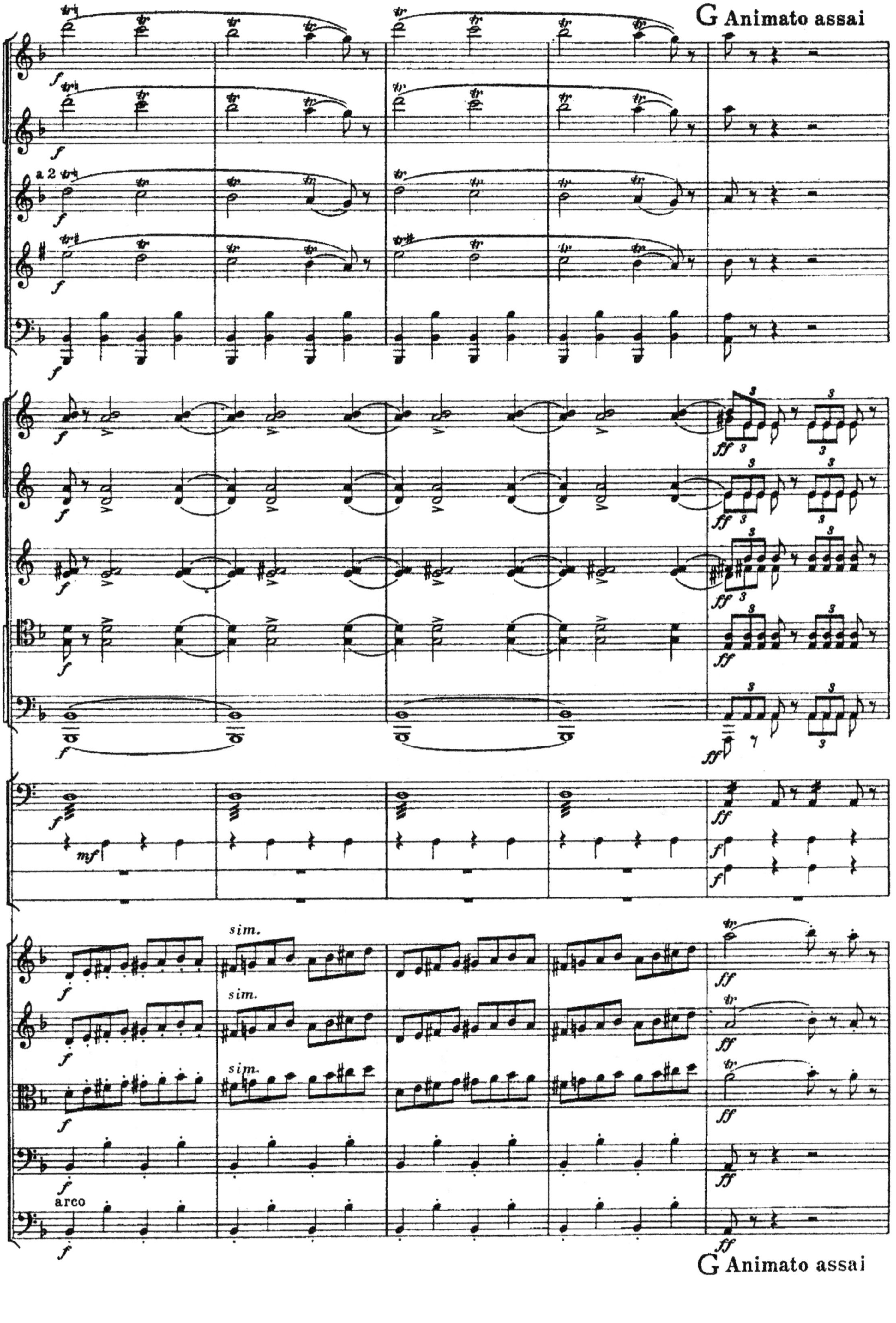
G Animato assai
a 2
sim.
sim.
sim.
arco
G Animato assai

muta in A

Cor. I. II
Cor. III. IV
Trbe. I. II
Vle.
[sim.]
Vcell.
Cb.
Fl.
a 2
Ob.
Clar. in A
Fag.
Viol. I
con sordini
Viol. II
pizz.

poco rit.

Vle. con sordini

mf

dim. poco a poco

poco rit.

H Più sostenuto

baguette (палочкой)

Piatti

col legno

col legno

H Più sostenuto

a 2
p
a 2
p
a 2
p
p
sim.
p+
p
arco
p
pp
pp
col legno
p
p
poco cresc.
poco cresc.
poco cresc.
poco cresc.
poco cresc.
poco cresc.
poco cresc.
poco cresc.
poco cresc.
poco cresc.

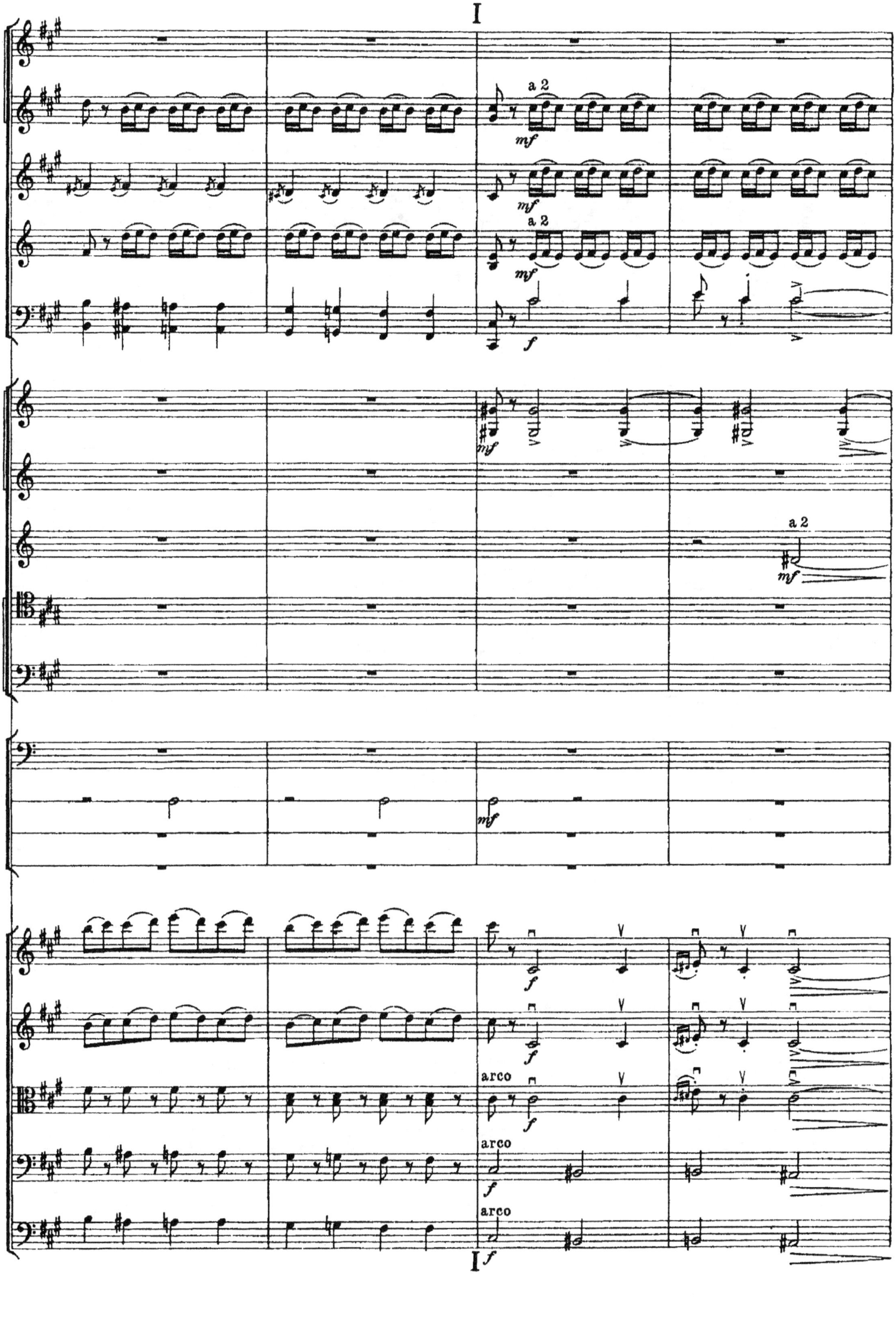
I
a 2
mf
f
arco
I

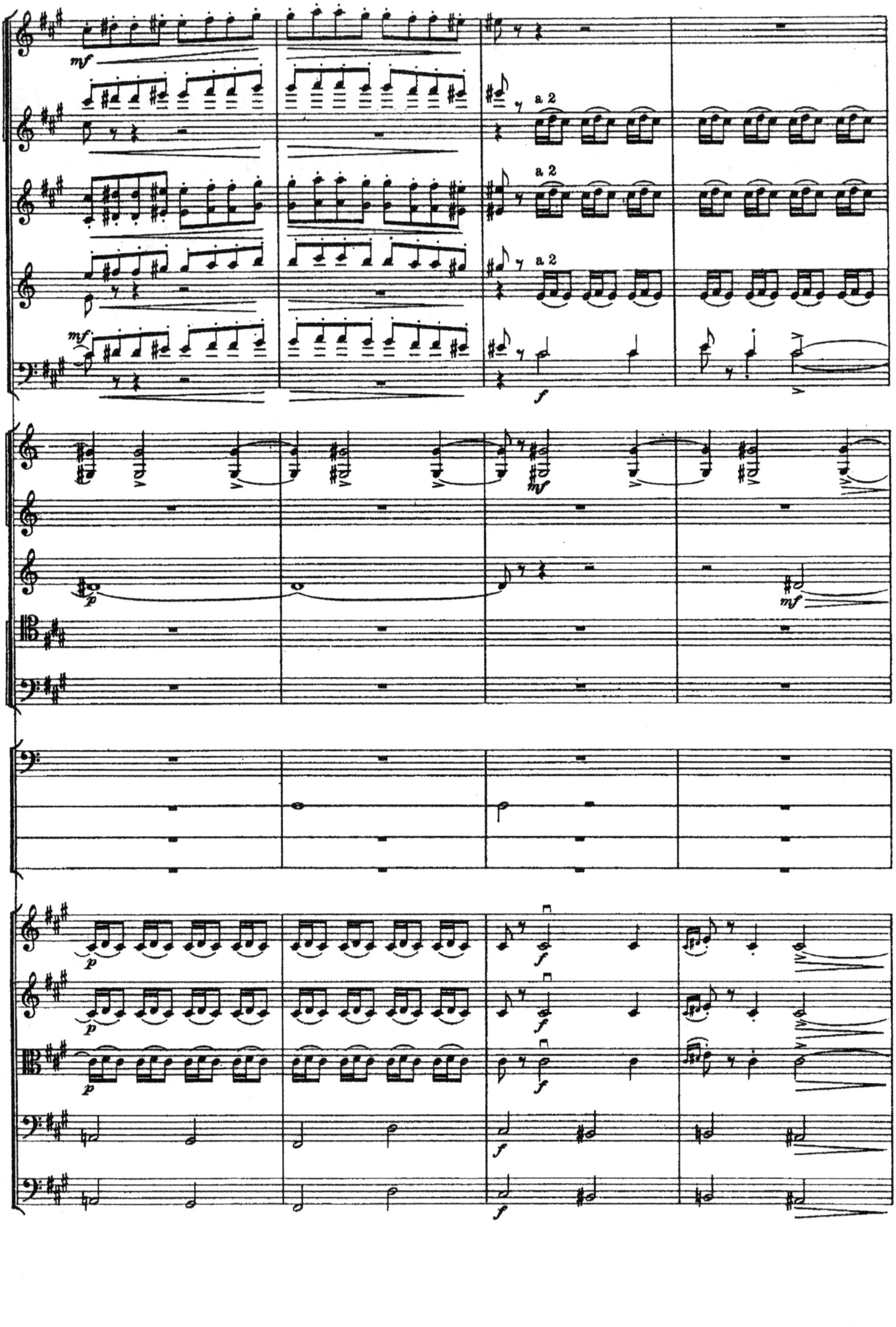
a 2
a 2
a 2

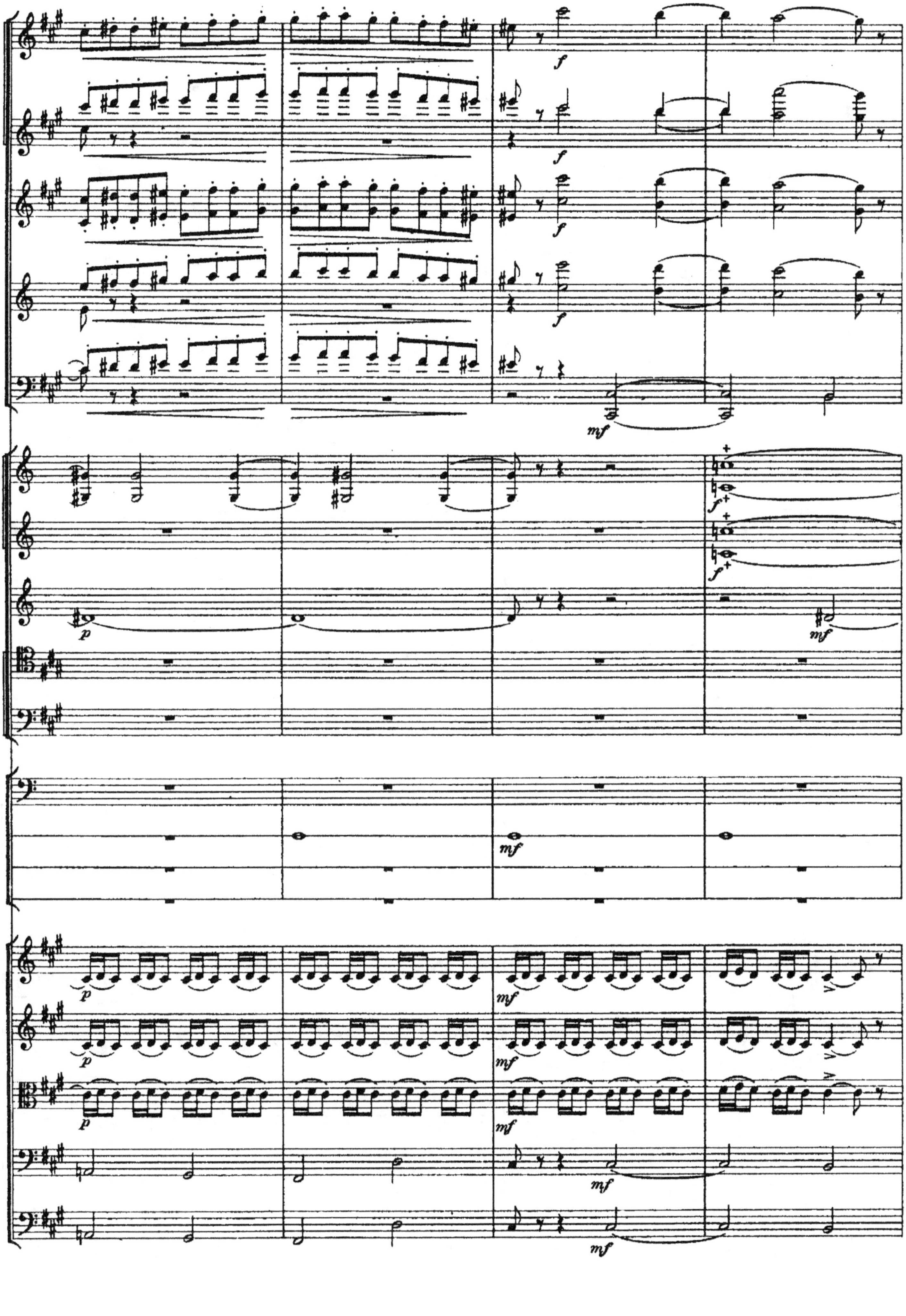

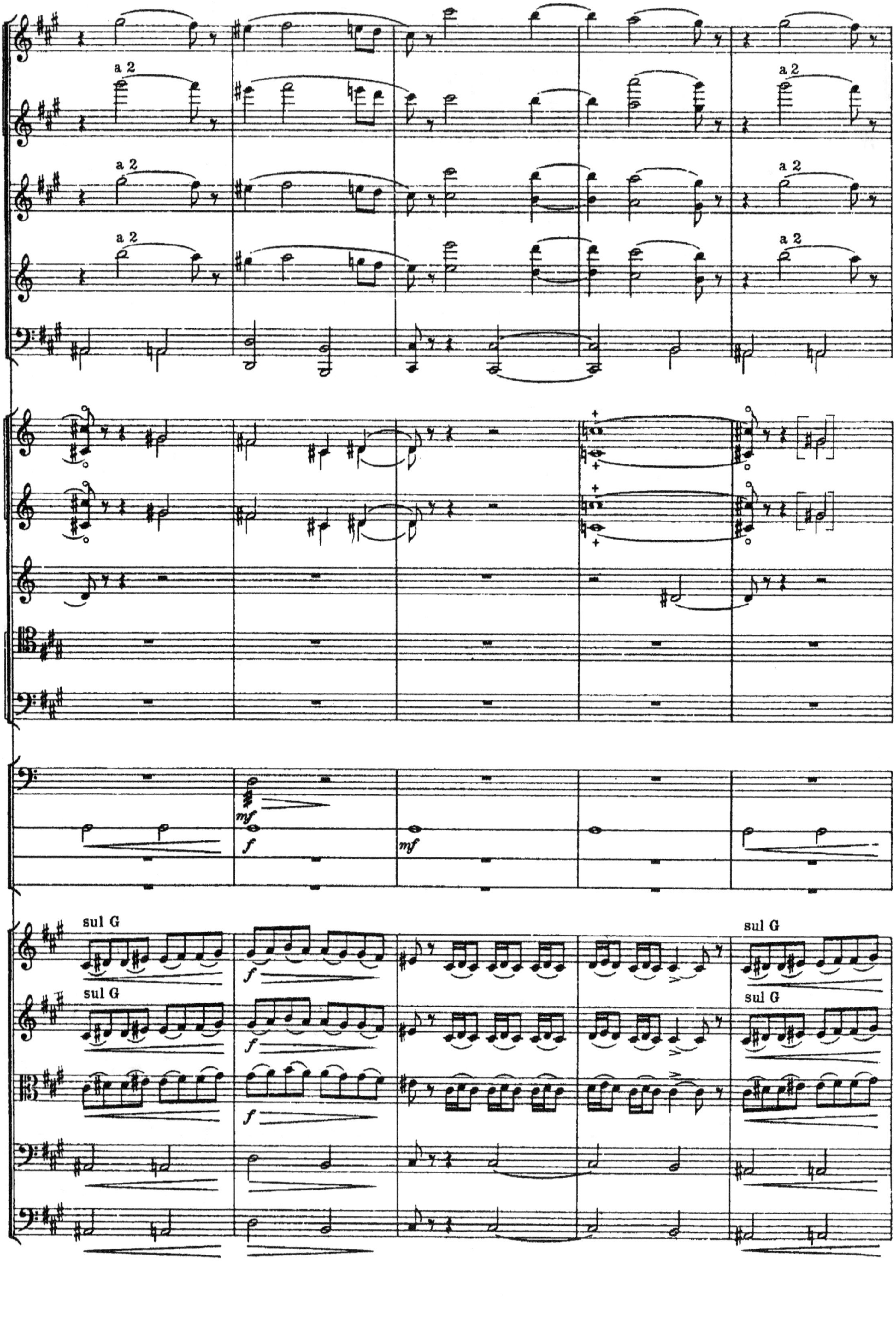
a 2
a 2
a 2
a 2
a 2
a 2
mf
f
mf
sul G
sul G
sul G
sul G
f
f
f

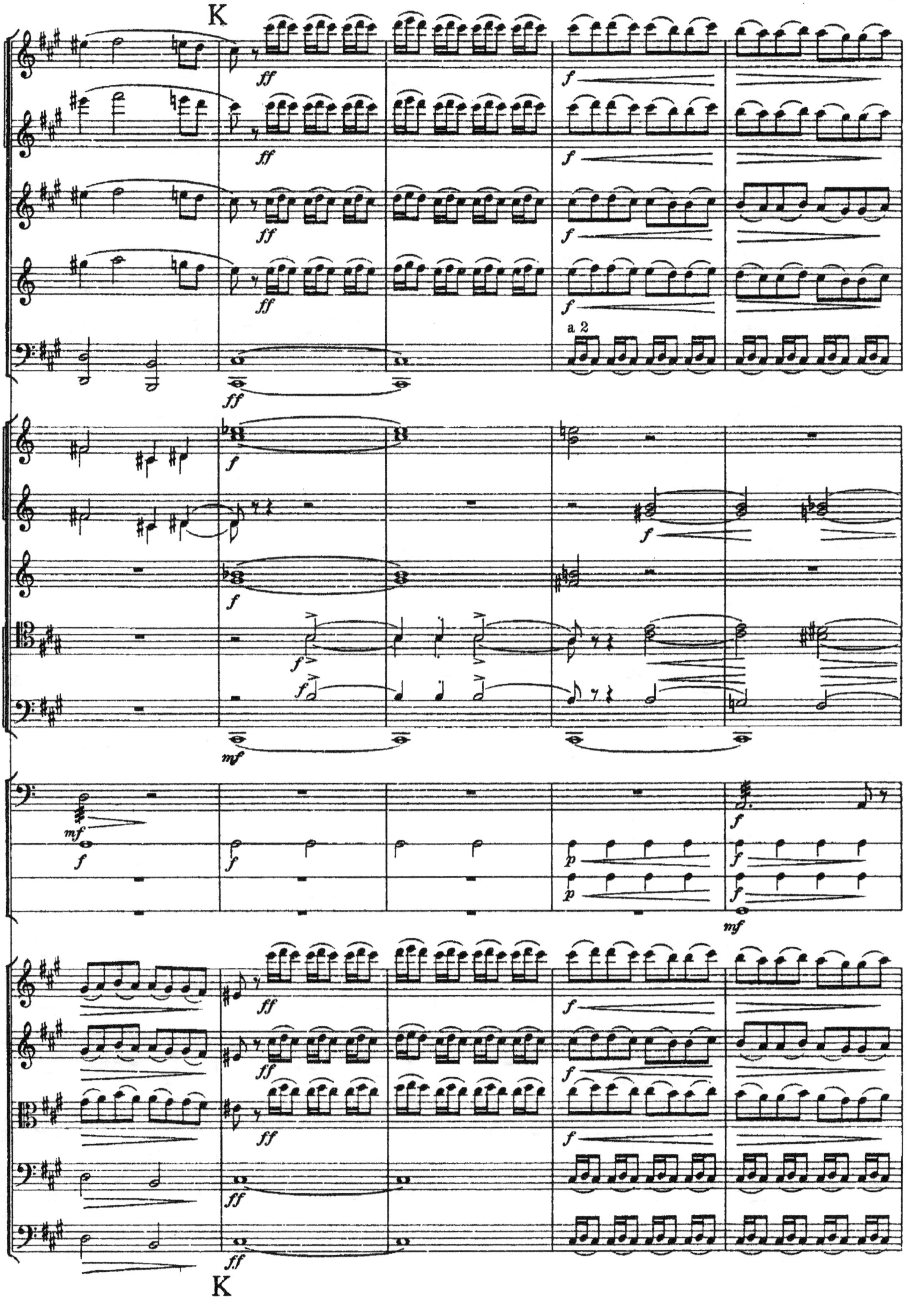
K
a 2
K

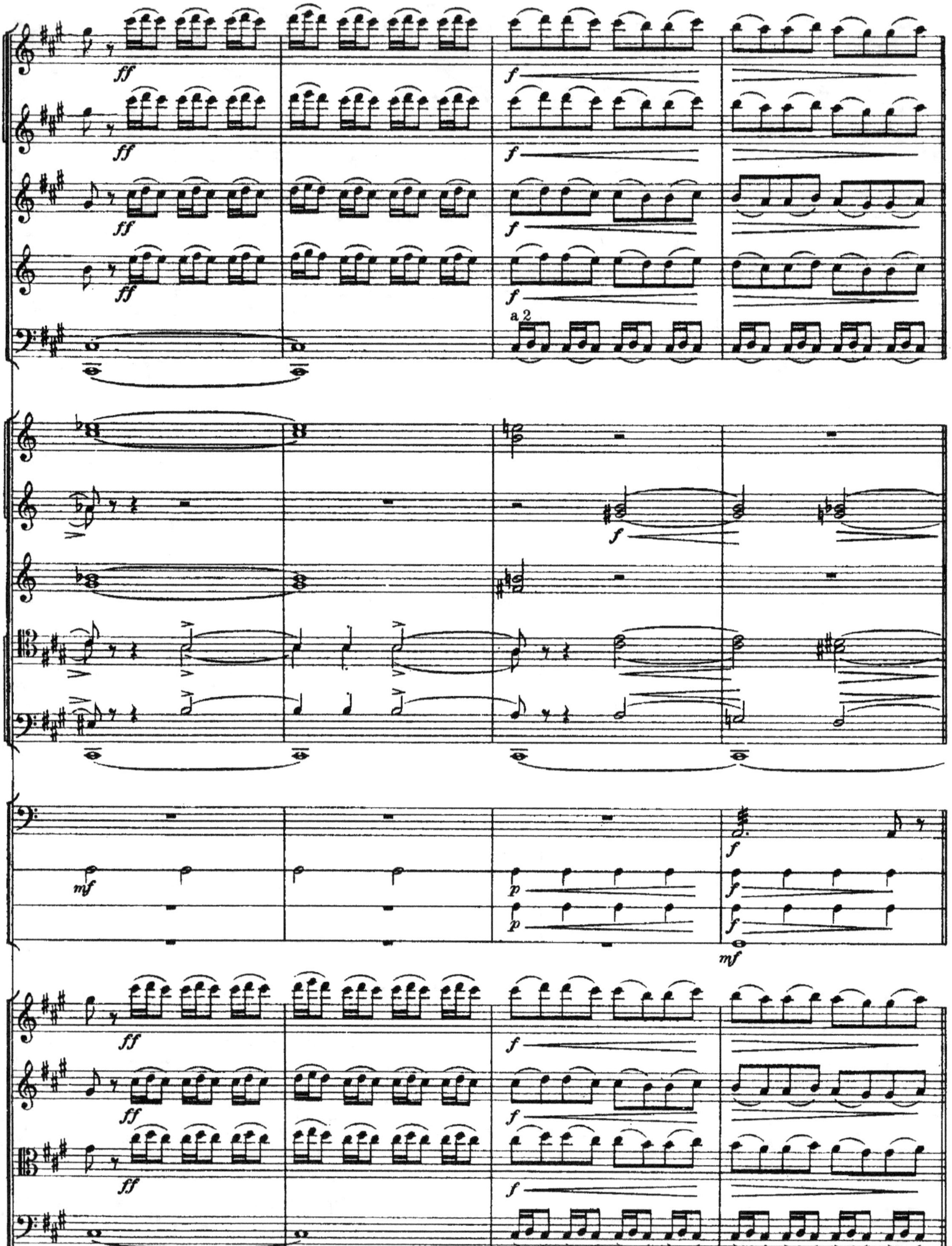
a 2

L Tempo I (Allegro feroce)

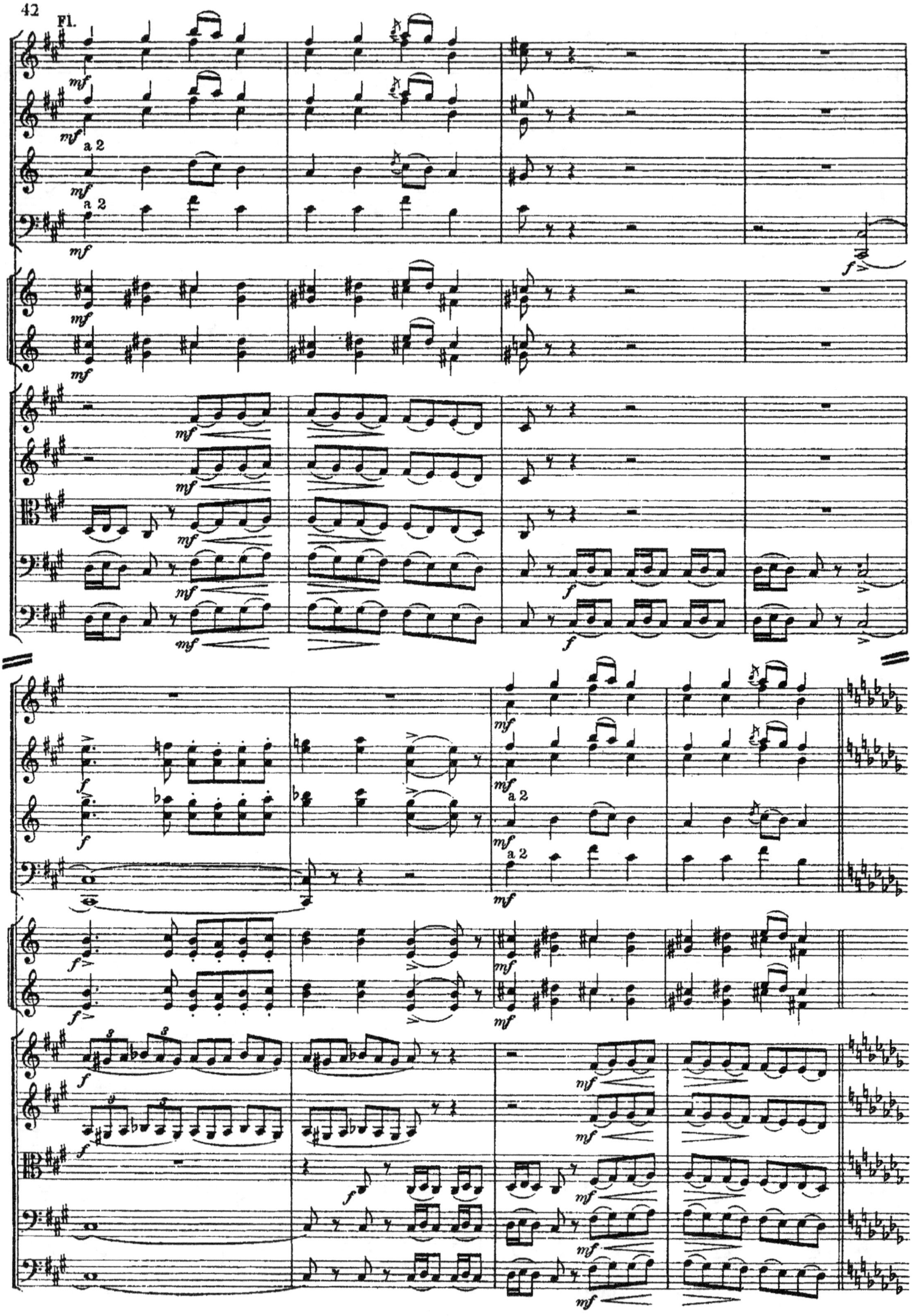
Fl.
a 2
a 2
a 2
a 2

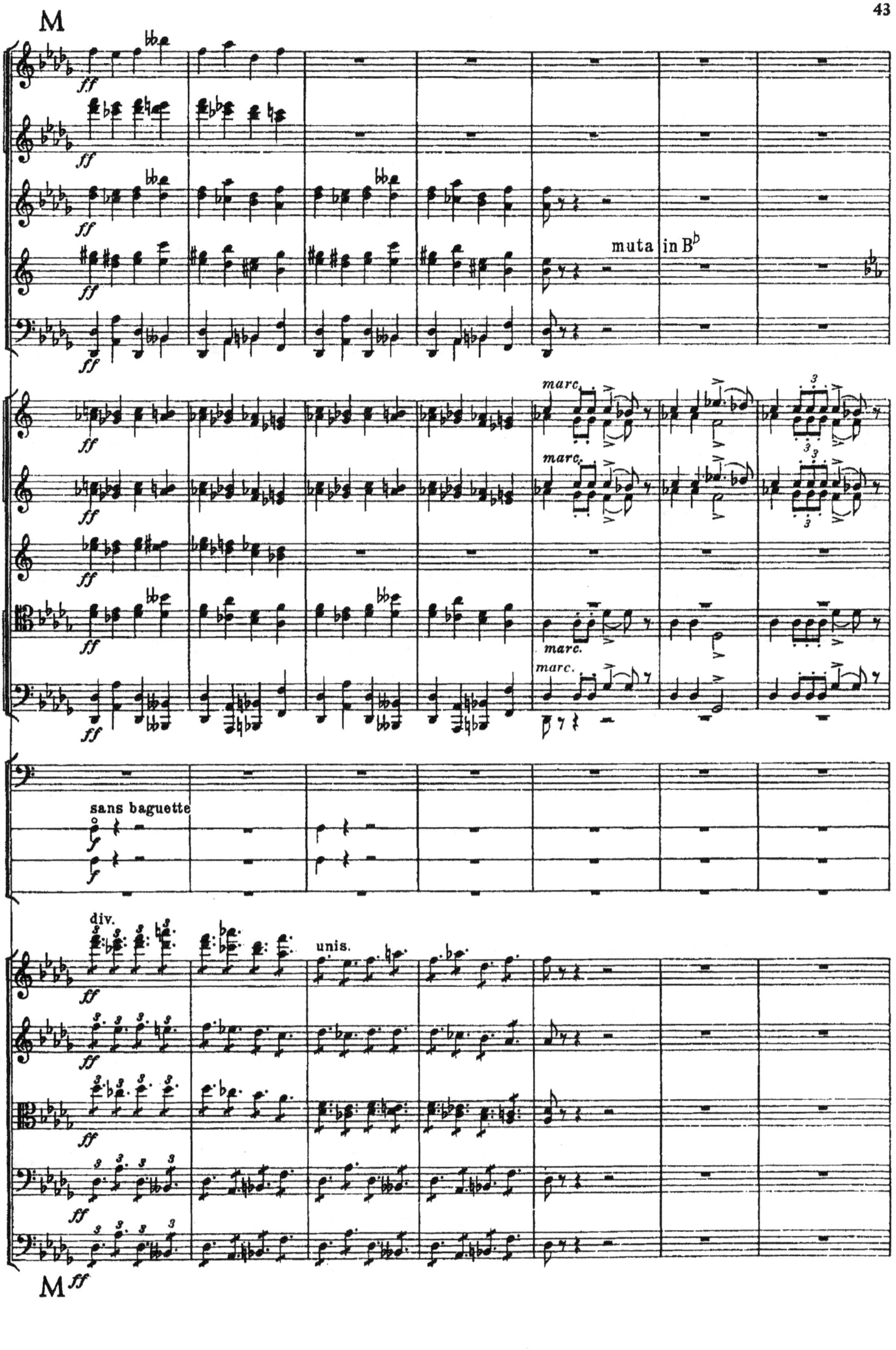
M
ff
muta in B♭
marc.
sans baguette
div.
unis.
M

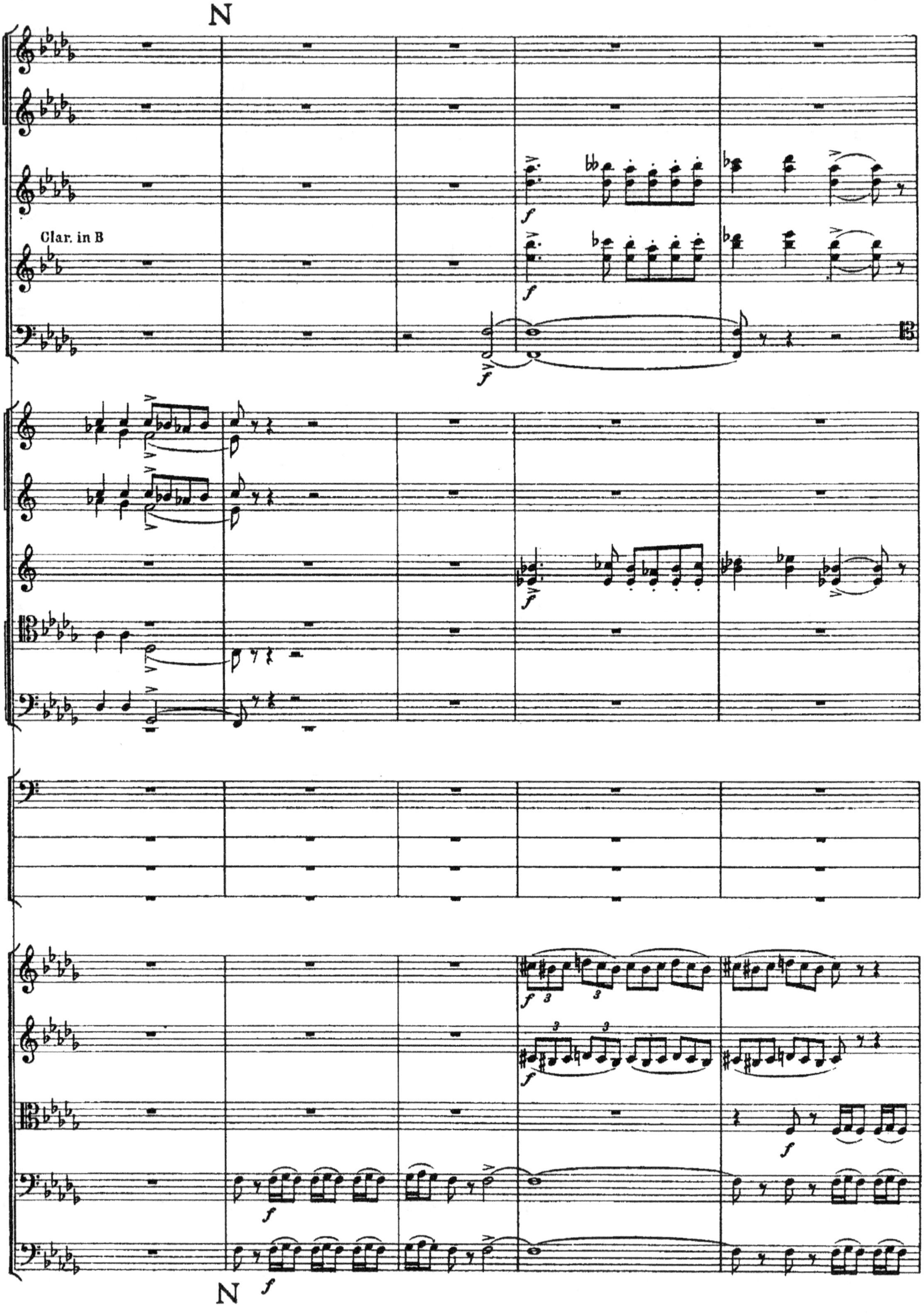
N
Clar. in B
f
N

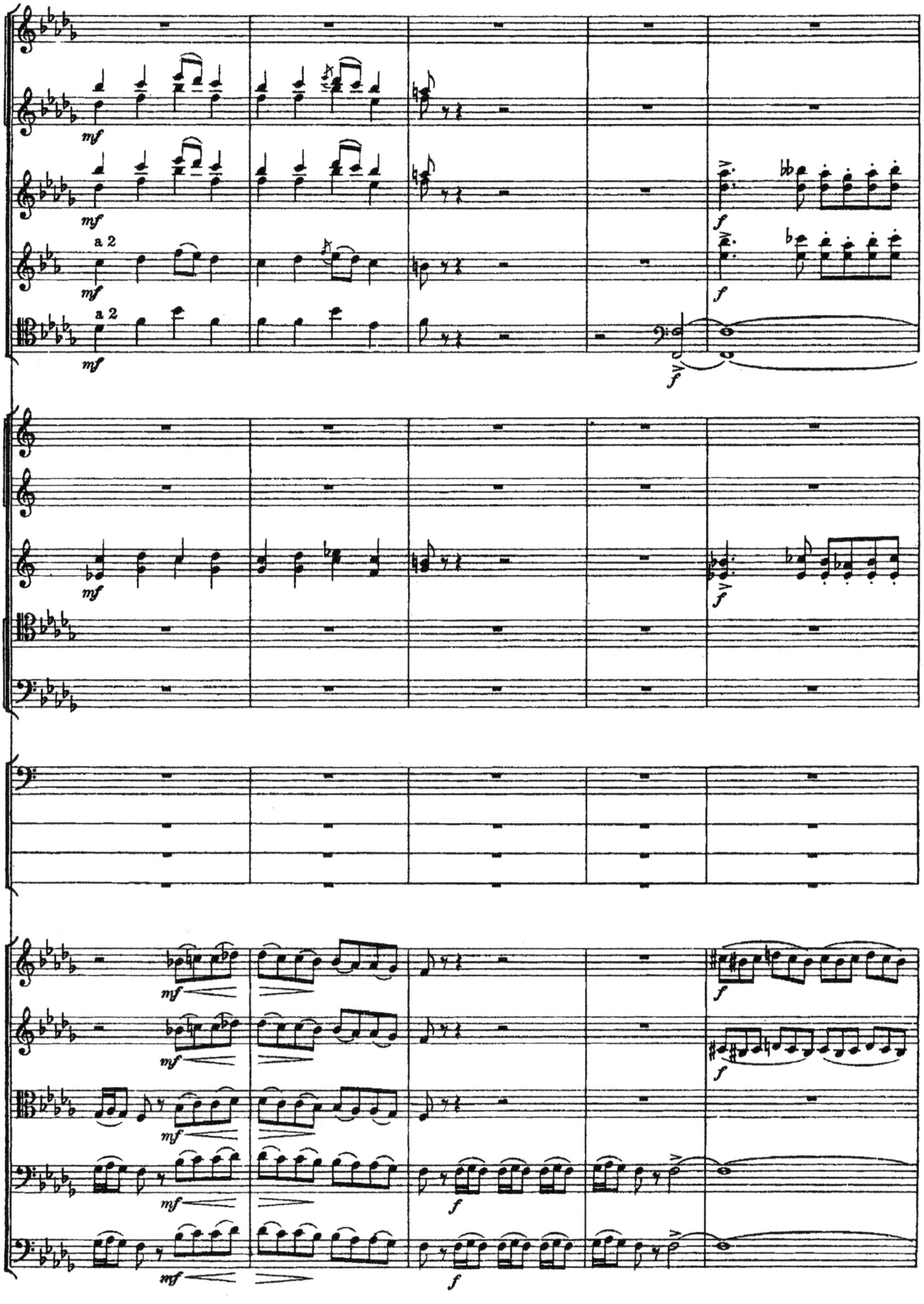
a 2
a 2

Sostenuto
Pesante

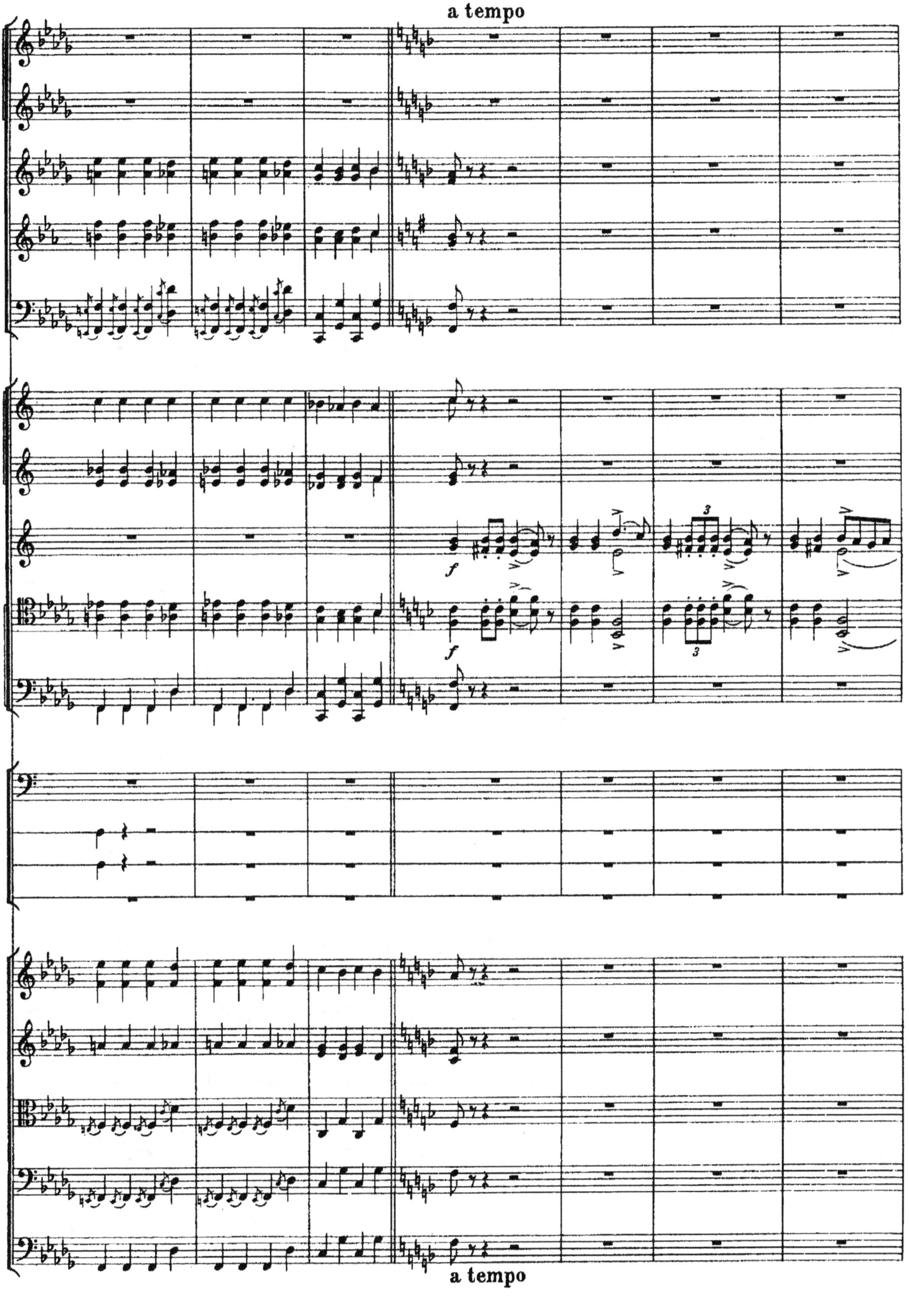
a tempo
f
f
3
3
a tempo

P
a 2
a 2
a 2
a 2
pizz.
pizz.
pizz.
pizz.
pizz.
arco
arco
arco
arco
arco
P

mf
mf
f
f
f
f
mf
mf
pizz.
arco
f
f
f
pizz.
arco
f
f
f
pizz.
arco
f
f
f
pizz.
arco
f
f
f
pizz.
arco
f
f
f

50

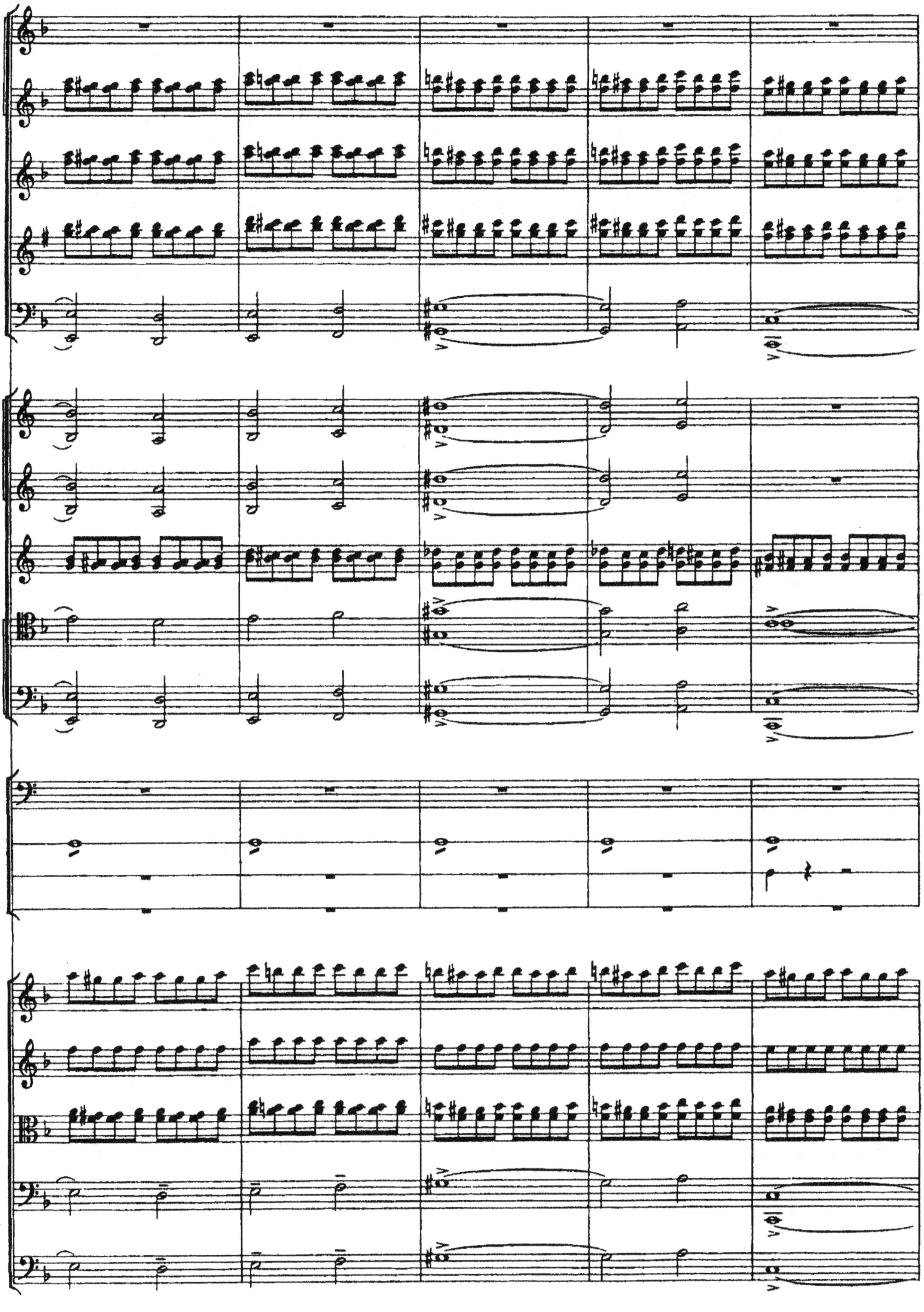

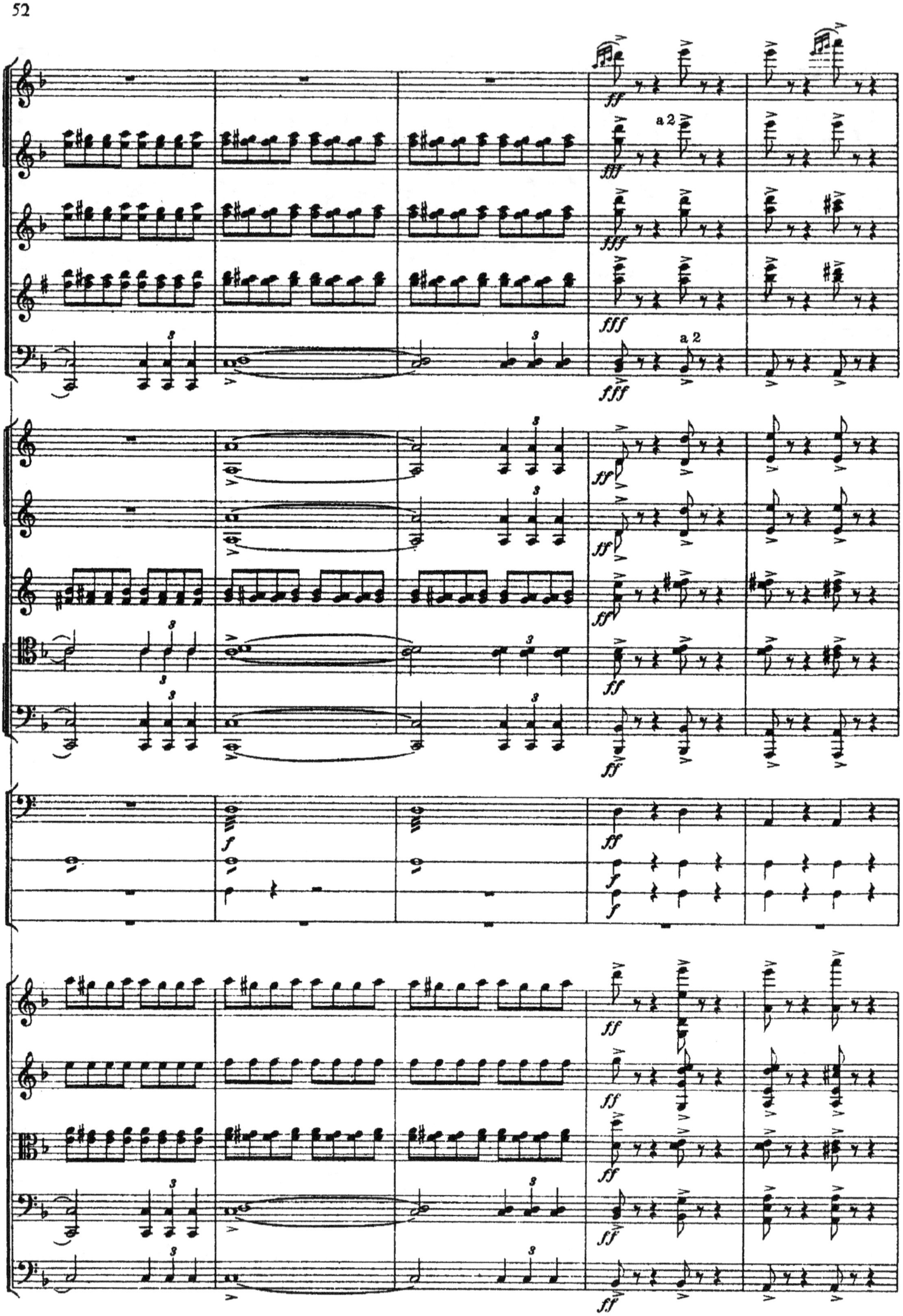
a 2
ff
fff
f

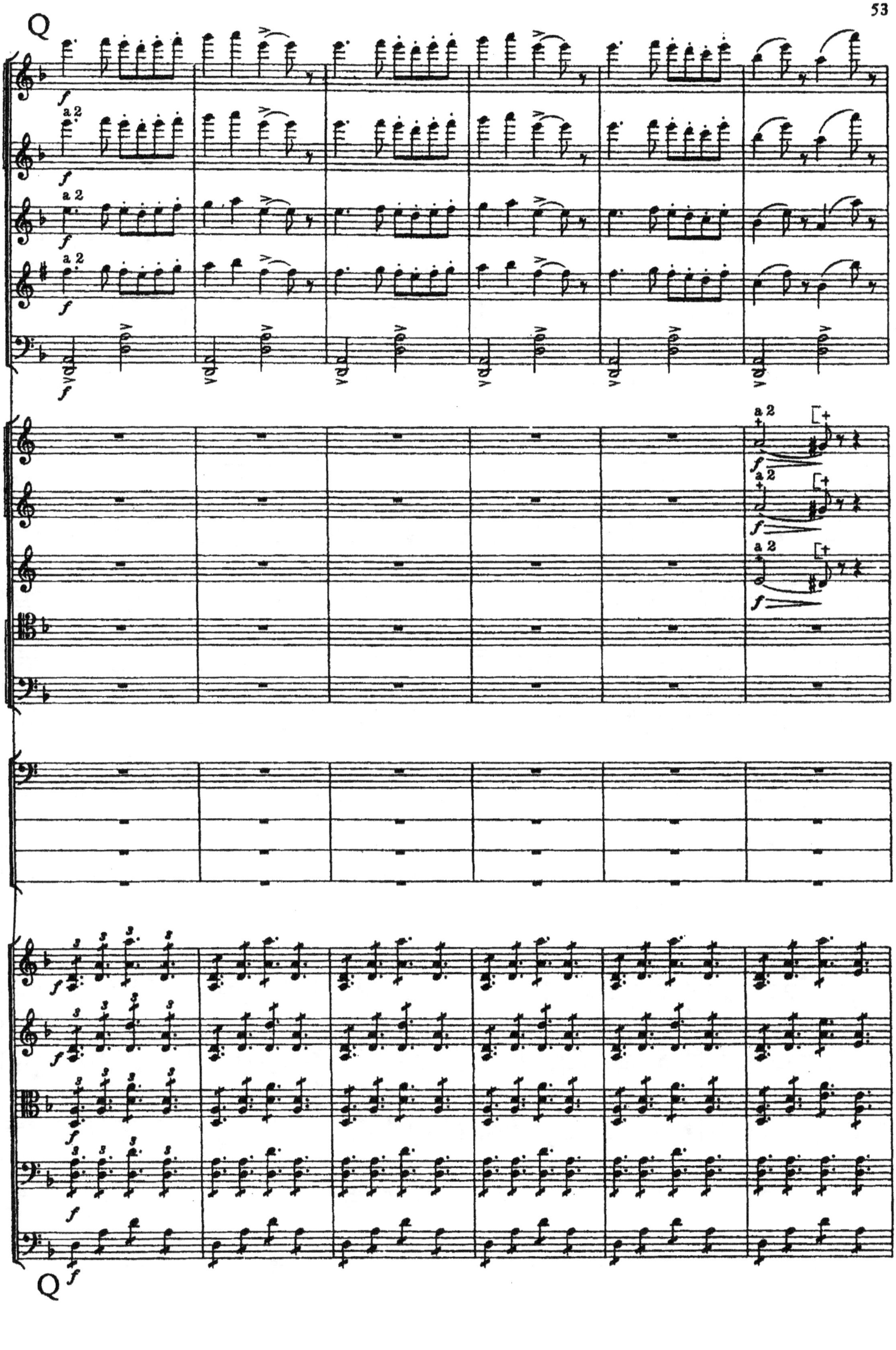
Q
a 2
a 2
a 2
a 2
a 2
a 2
Q

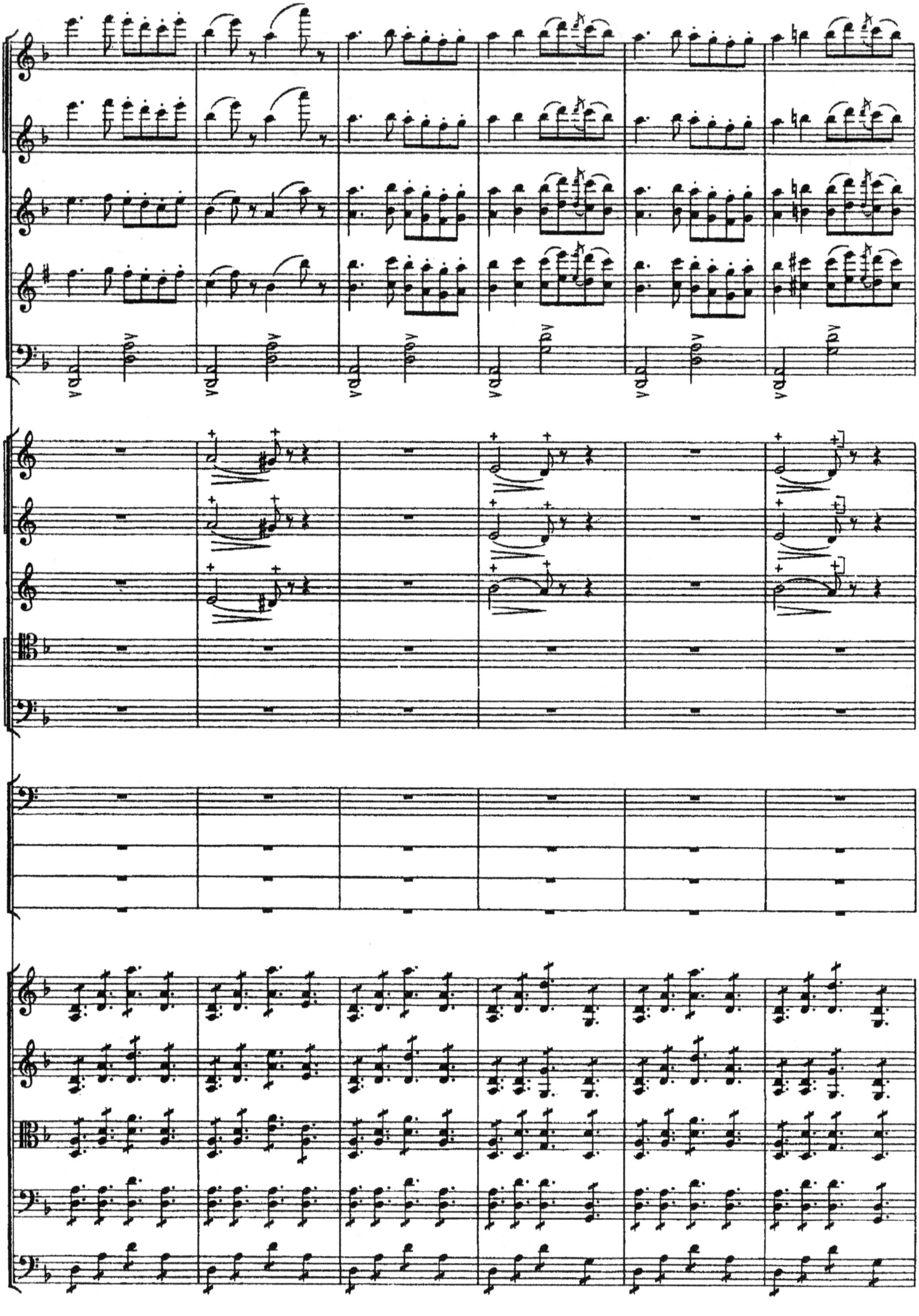

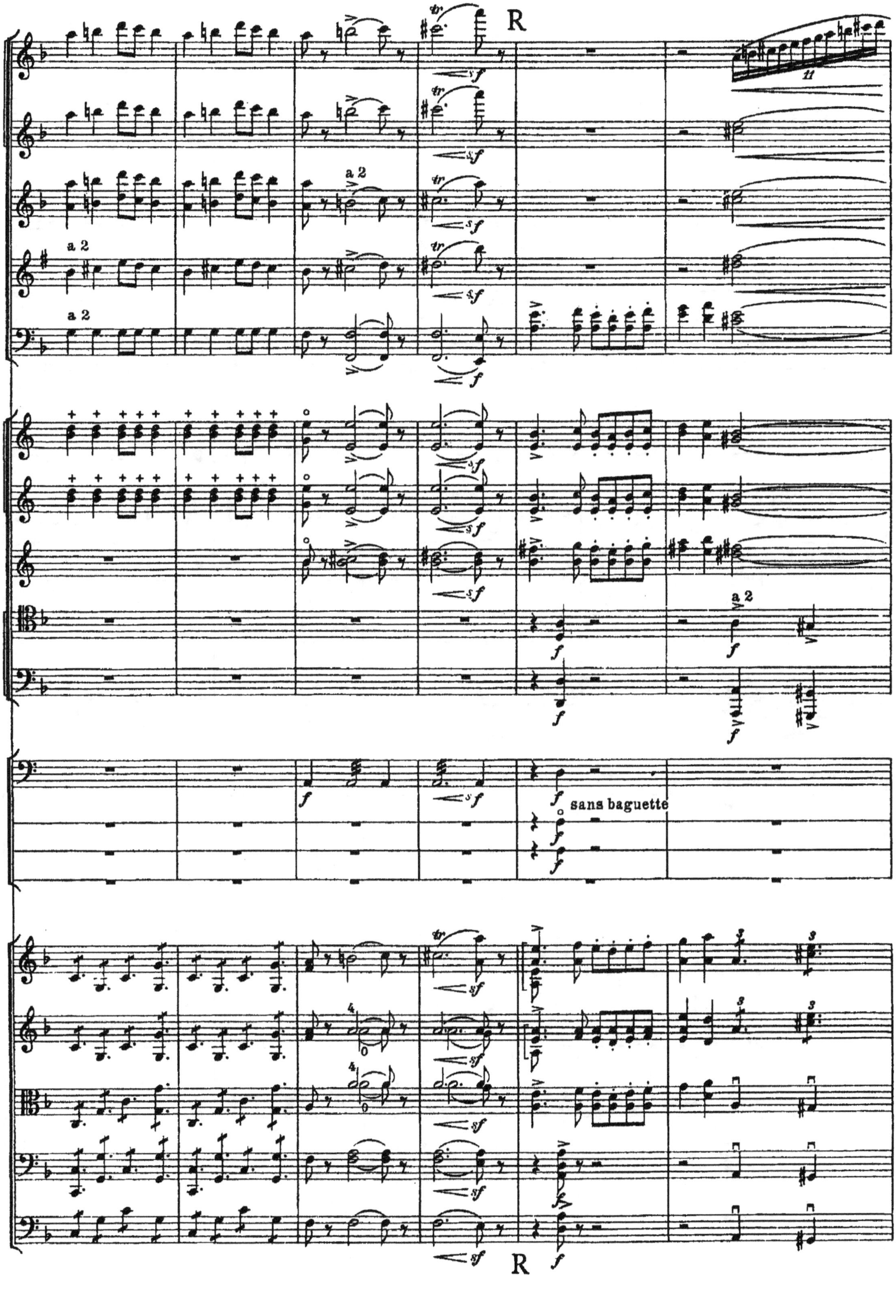
R
a 2
a 2
a 2
a 2
sans baguette
R

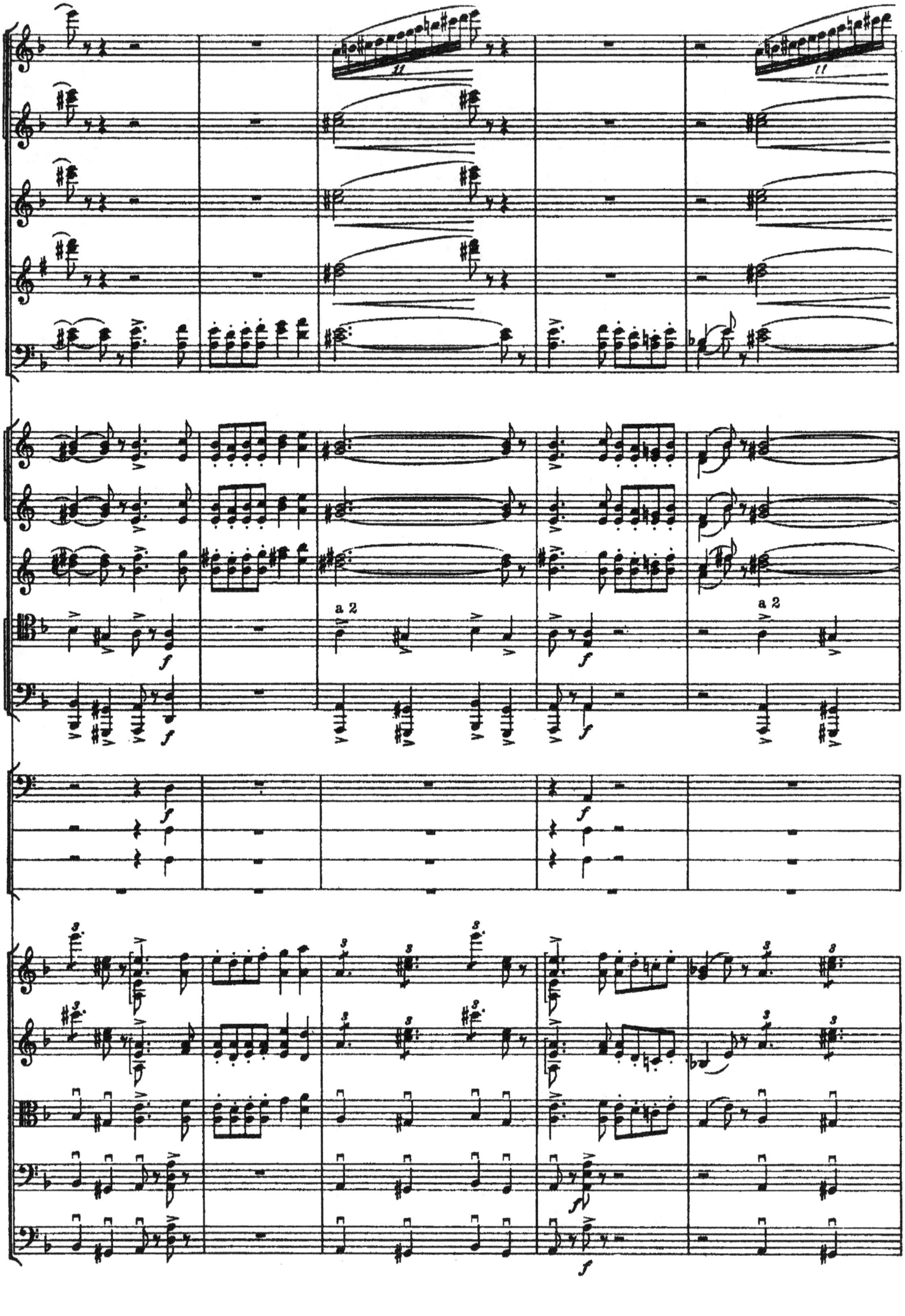
a 2
a 2

a 2
p cresc.
p cresc.
p cresc.
a 2
f
f
f
p cresc.
p cresc.
p cresc.
p cresc.
f
f

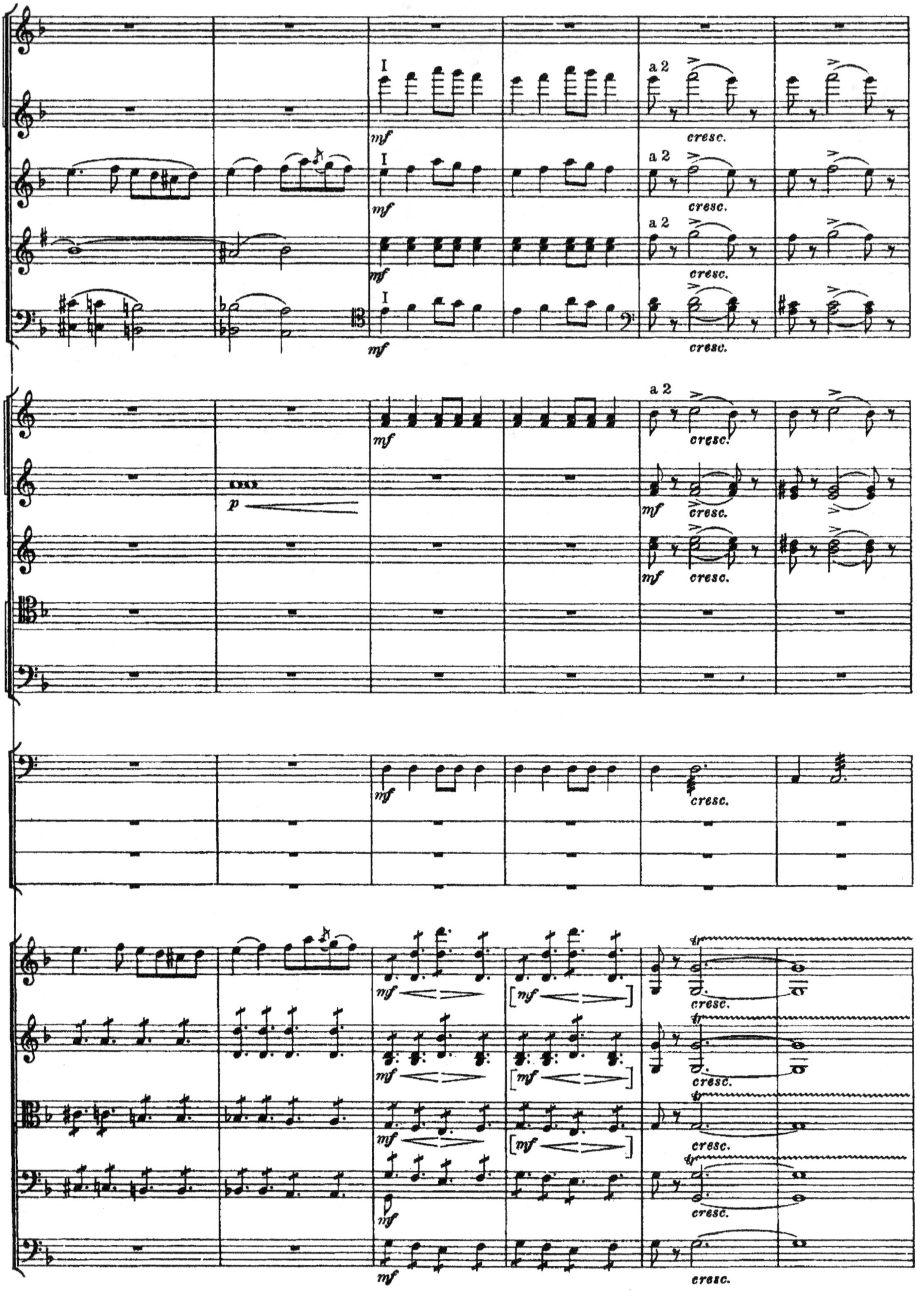
I
mf
a 2
cresc.
p
tr

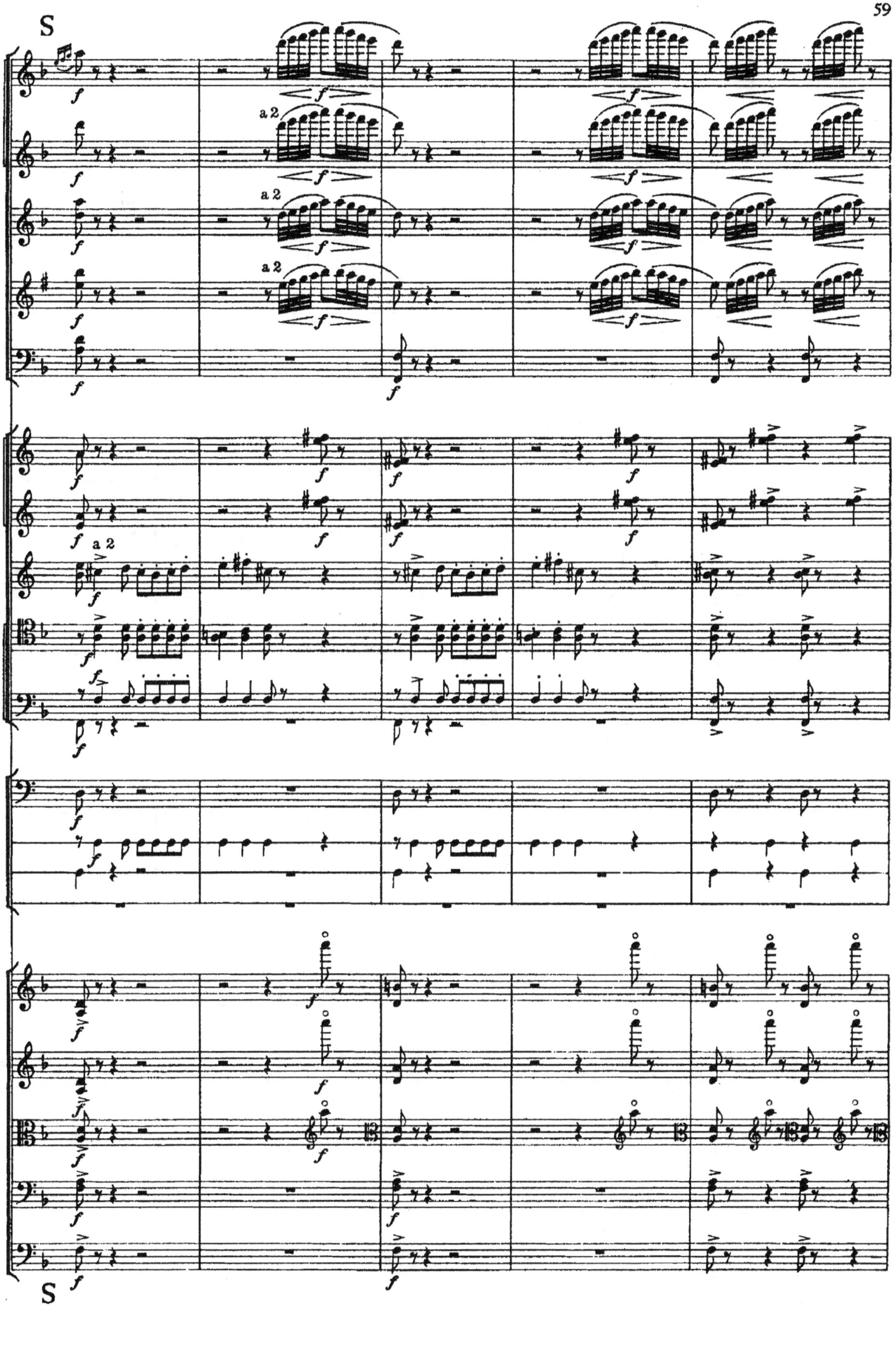
S
a 2
f
S

muta in A

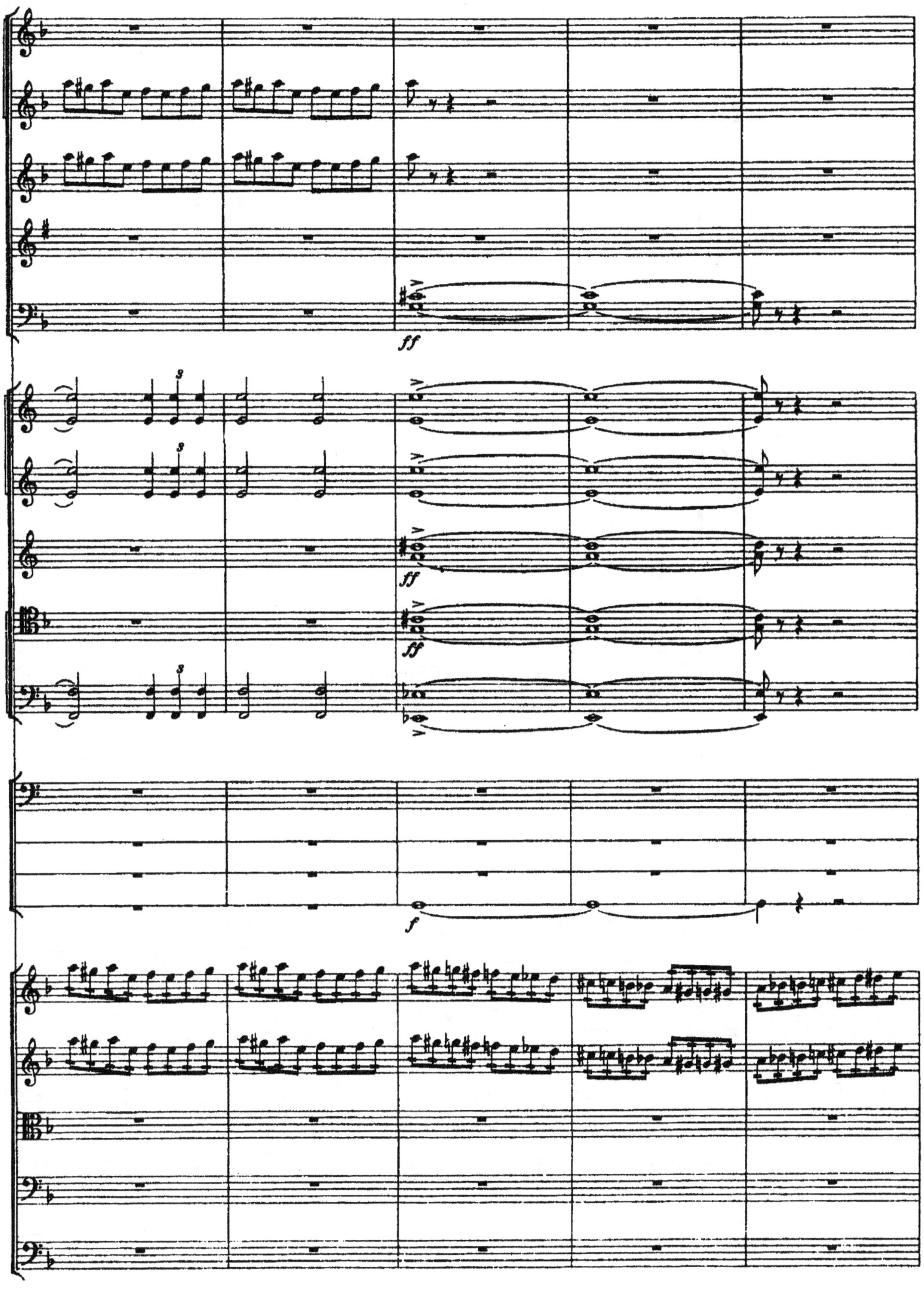

3
ff
f

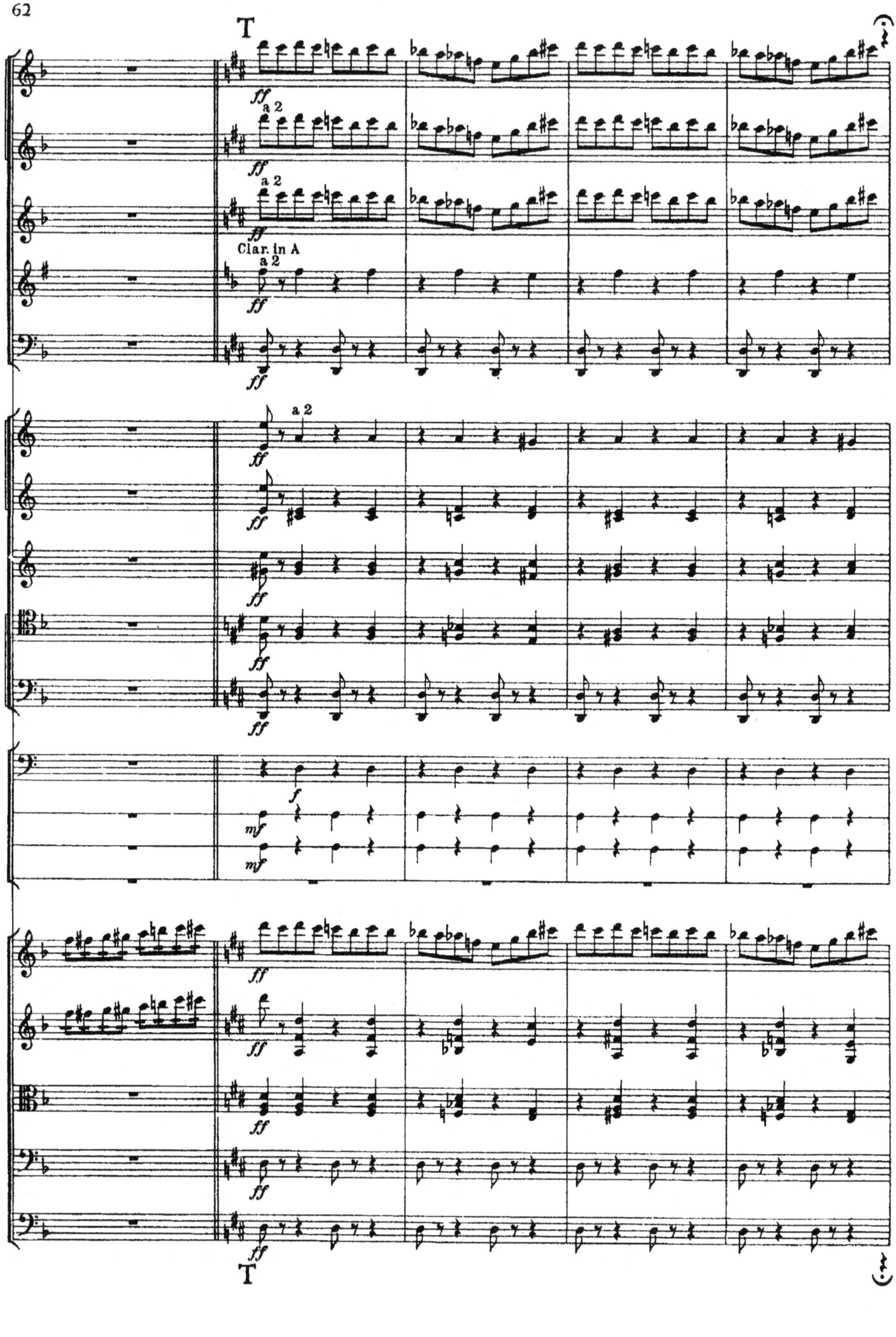
T
ff
a 2
Clar. in A
f
mf
T

Poco più sostenuto

Poco più sostenuto

64

poco a poco più animato

poco a poco più animato

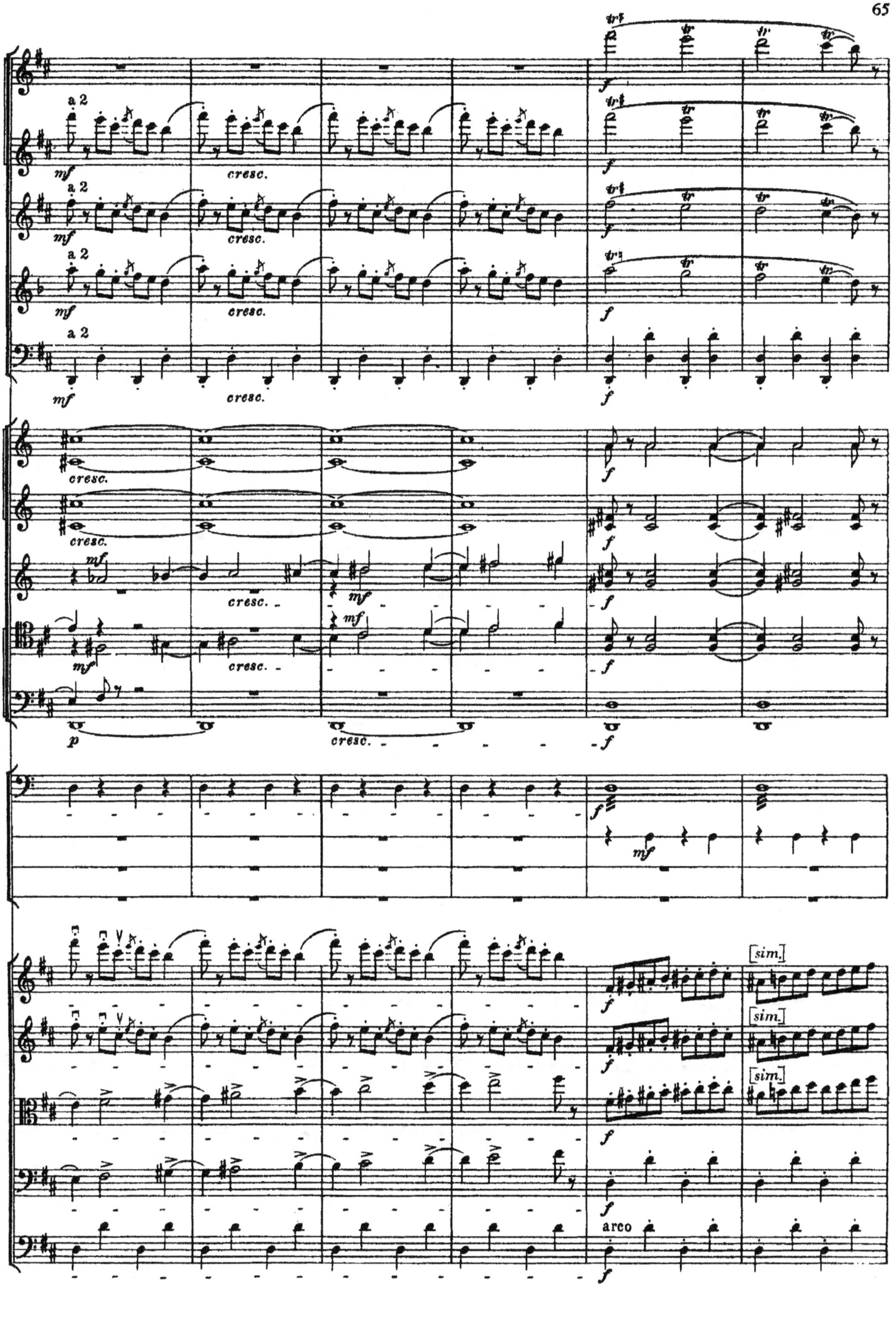
a 2
mf
cresc.
f
p
arco
[sim.]

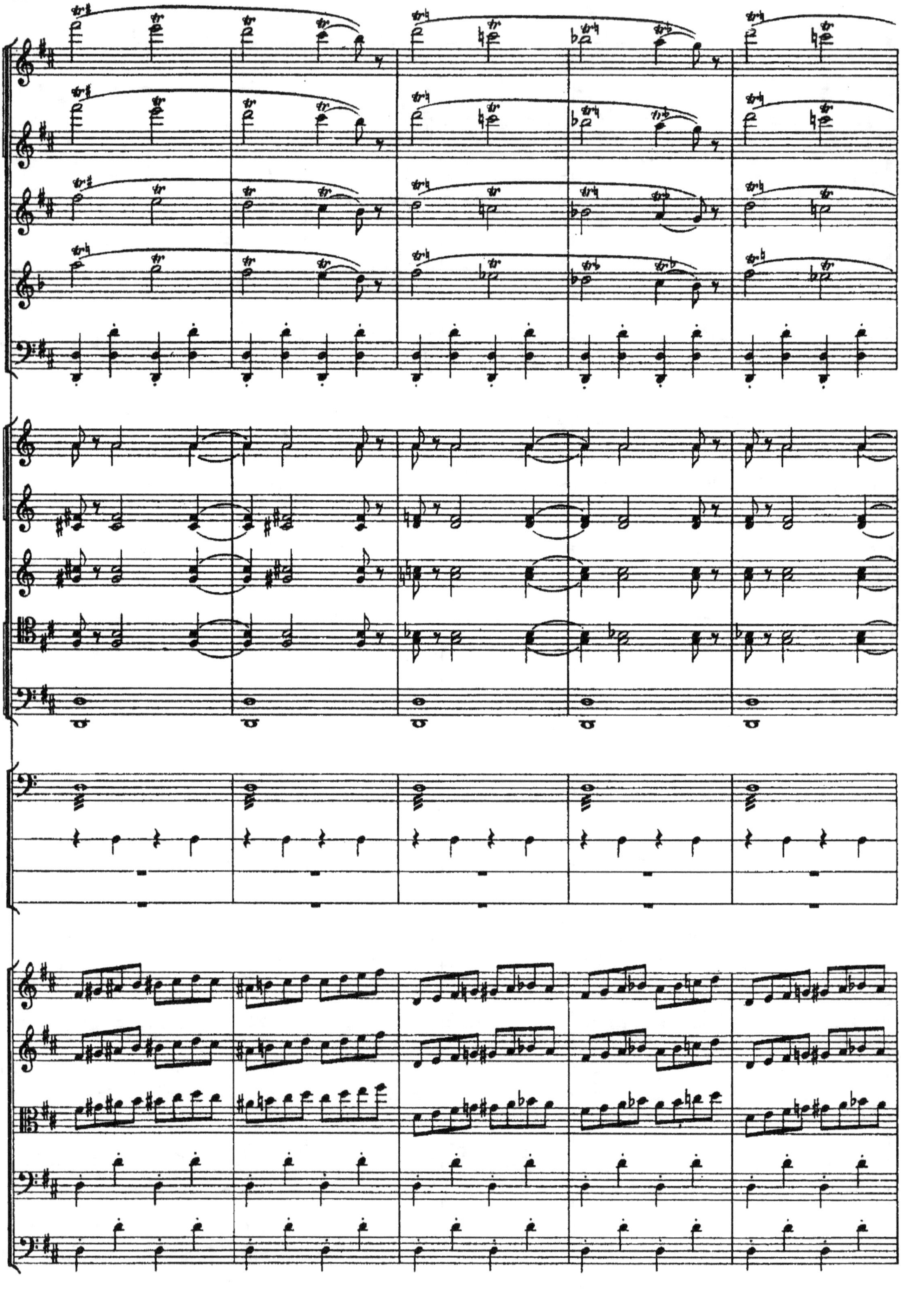
tr

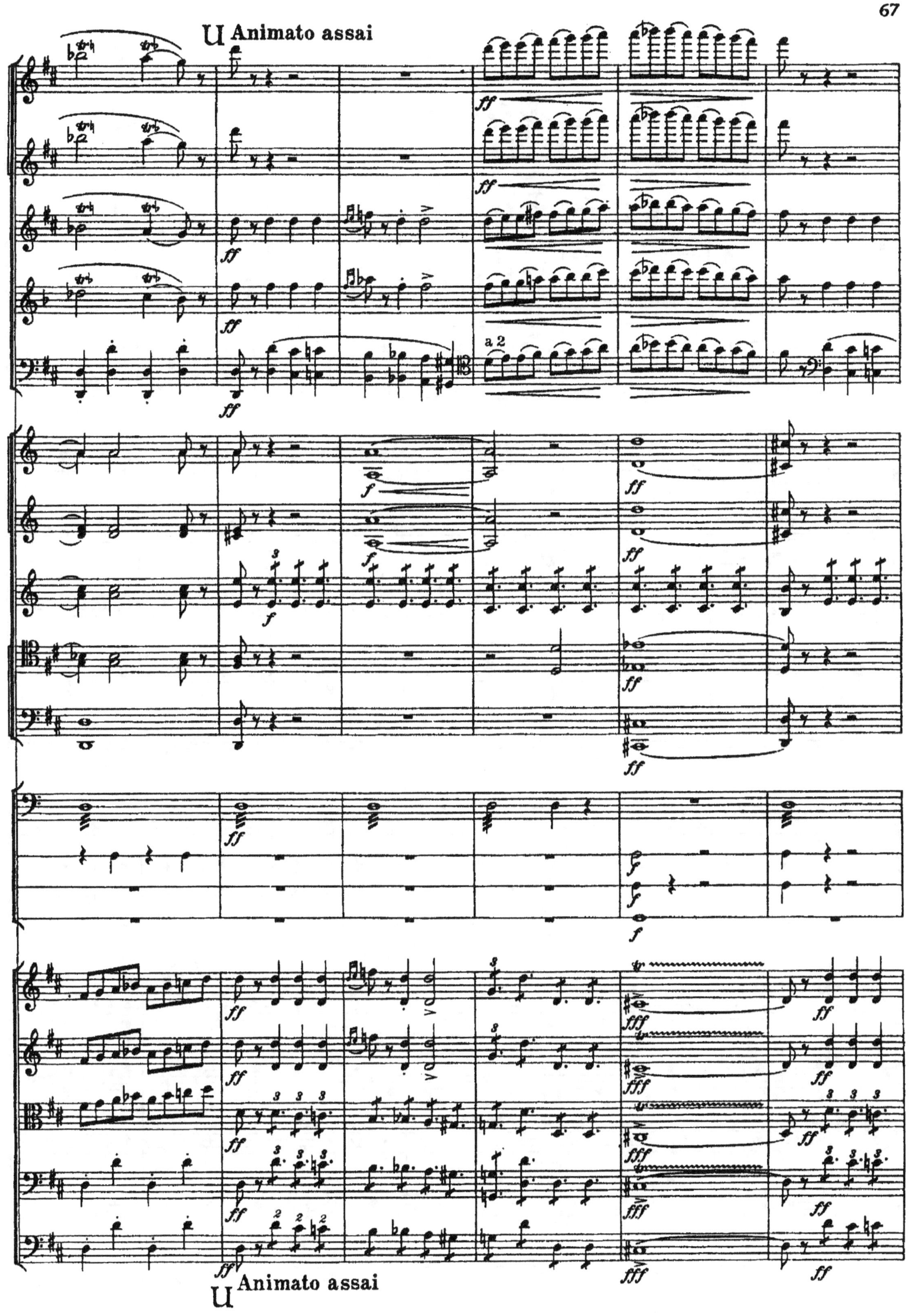
U Animato assai
a 2
ff
f
fff
U Animato assai

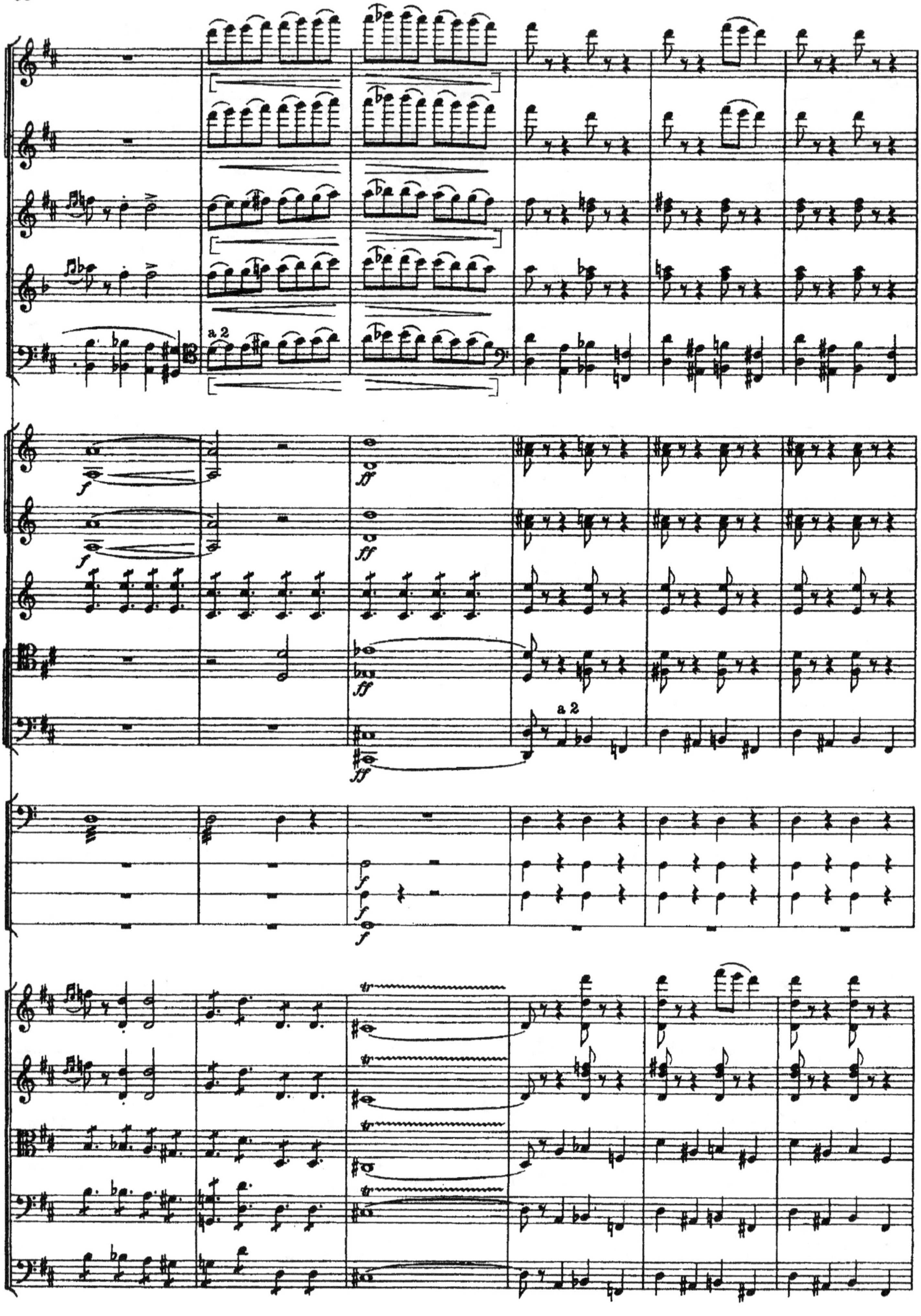
a 2
f
ff
a 2
f
f
f
tr

muta in B♭

Tacet al Fine

Tacet al Fine

Tacet al Fine

Tacet al Fine

(baguette)

Tacet al Fine

Tacet al Fine

Tacet al Fine

dim. assai

dim. assai

S'il est impossible de procurer une cloche en re on ne la doit remplacer par aucun autre instrument.

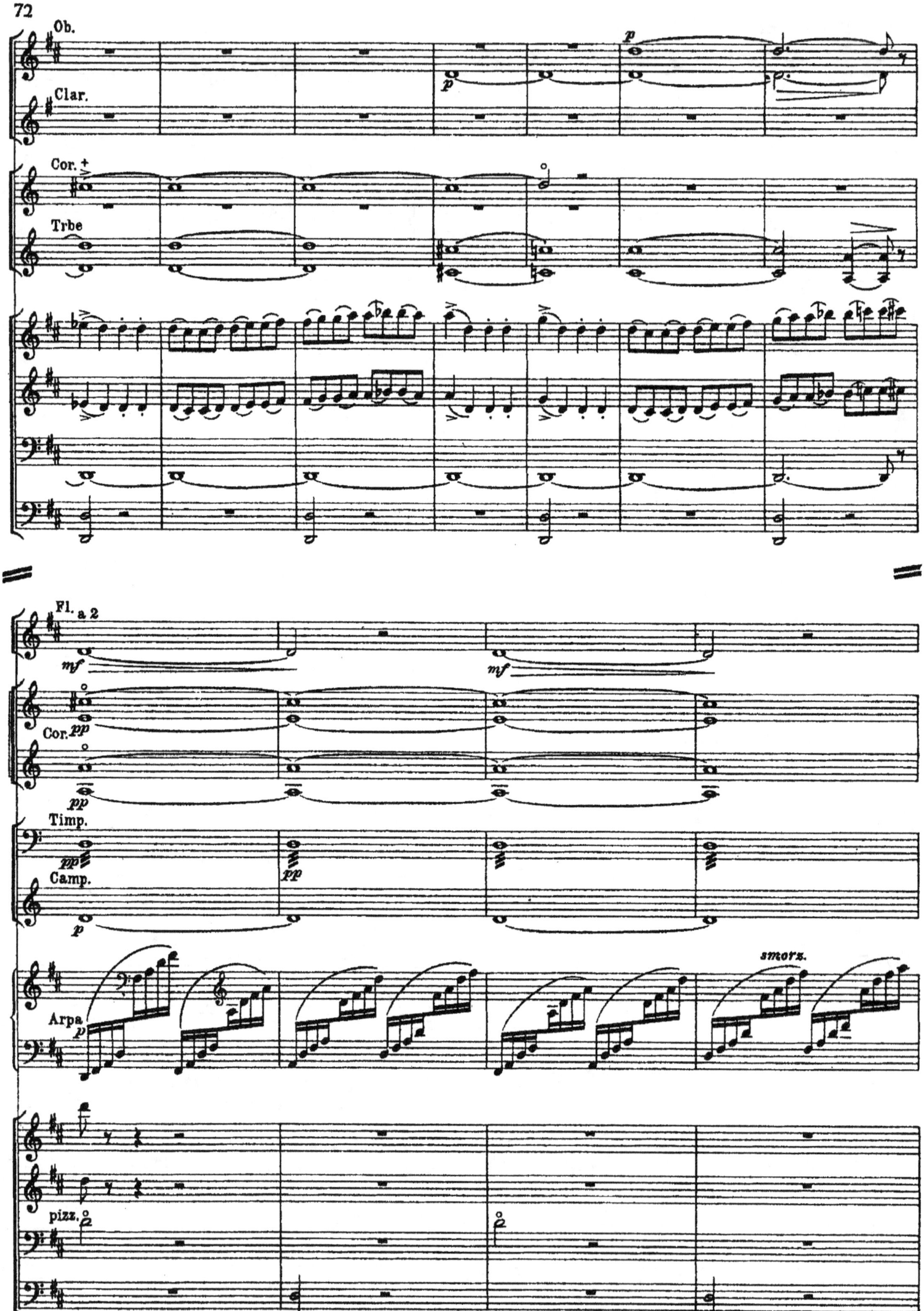
Ob.
Clar.
Cor.
Trbe
Fl. a 2
Cor.
Timp.
Camp.
Arpa
smorz.
pizz.

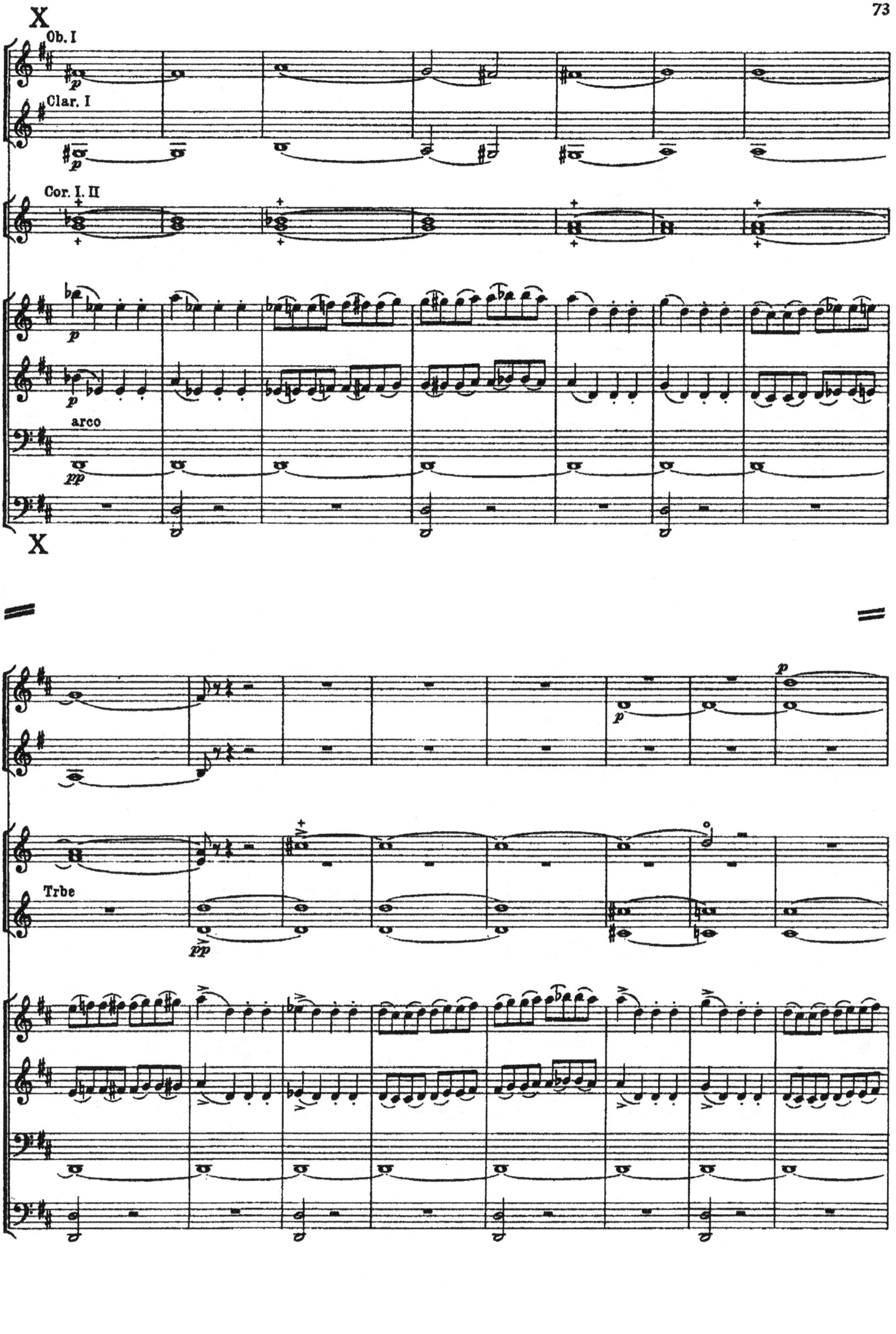
X
Ob. I
p
Clar. I
p
Cor. I. II
p
arco
pp
X
p
p
Trbe
pp

Y Meno mosso. Tranquillo

Y Meno mosso. Tranquillo

Z Solo
a 2
mf dim.
dolce
pp
pp
ppp
p
p
smorz.
div.
arco
pizz.
mf
arco
pp
arco
ppp
pizz.
pp
Z
pp
perd.
a 2
p dim.
pp
pp
ppp
p
p
pizz.
mf
arco
pp

p
pp
pp
ppp
smorz.
p dim.
8
div.
pp
div.
pp
pizz.
pp
arco
pp
pizz.
p
pizz.
pp
pp